The Contemporary Explosion of Theology

Langdon Gilkey; Hans Küng; Teilhard de Chardin;
Norman Pittenger; John Cobb; Edward Schillebeeckx;
Jürgen Moltmann; Henry Cade; Richard Rubenstein;
Elie Wiesel and Emil Fackenheim

Ecumenical Studies in Theology

Edited and Introduced by

MICHAEL D. RYAN

The Scarecrow Press, Inc.
Metuchen, N. J.   1975

The Scripture quotations in this publication are from The Revised Standard Version Bible and are used by permission.

Acknowledgments for the copyrighted materials reprinted here as studies will be found at the beginning of each selection.

Acknowledgments for copyrighted brief quotations will be found in the footnotes.

Library of Congress Cataloging in Publication Data

Ryan, Michael D   comp.
    The contemporary explosion of theology.

    Includes index.
    1. Theology, Doctrinal.   2. Theology, Doctrinal—
History—20th century. I. Gilkey, Langdon Brown,
1919-   II. Title.
BT75.2.R9   230'.09'04   74-34125
ISBN 0-8108-0794-7

For J. C. Brown and Frank Jannuzi
who in retirement discovered a
new vocation as theologians

CONTENTS

Preface   vii
Introduction and Background   1

PART I: THEOLOGY IN CRISIS   19

Study 1. Langdon Gilkey, The Crisis of the Word
"God"   20
The Crisis of "God" Language, by Langdon
Gilkey   27

Study 2. Hans Küng, The Crisis of Authority   34
The Holy Spirit: The Basis for the Church's
Confession of Sin, by Hans Küng   42

PART II: THEOLOGIES OF EVOLUTIONARY CHANGE   53

Study 3. Teilhard de Chardin, A Roman Catholic
Evolutionary Theology   54
The World, Man and God, by Teilhard de
Chardin   62

Study 4. Norman Pittenger and John Cobb,
Protestant Process Theology   71
Process-Thought and Christian Understanding,
by Norman Pittenger   75
The Divine Call into the Future, by John Cobb   84

PART III: THEOLOGIES OF THE FUTURE   87

Study 5. Edward Schillebeeckx, Christian Faith in
the Future   88
God as our Future, by Edward Schillebeeckx   92

Study 6. Jürgen Moltmann, Vision of Hope   100
The Gospel as Hope in History, by Jürgen
Moltmann   104

PART IV: THEOLOGIES OF THE HISTORICAL
            PRESENT   113

Study 7.   Henry Cade, Radical Christianity as
            Black Theology   114
    The Newly Emerging Black Church, by Henry
    Cade   120

Study 8.   Richard Rubenstein, The Holocaust and
            Radical Jewish Theology   130
    The Death Camps and the Decision of Faith,
    by Richard Rubenstein   134

Study 9.   Elie Wiesel and Emil Fackenheim, The
            Voice of the Holocaust   147
    Arrival at Auschwitz, by Elie Wiesel   150
    Commanded to Hope, by Emil Fackenheim   155

CONCLUSION: THEOLOGY IN THE NEW DIASPORA   163

Index   189

PREFACE

This book is designed as a series of introductory studies in theology for those who wish to take an ecumenical approach from the outset. It was produced as a result of not finding in print a volume which would serve as an introduction to the new trends in theology, and which would attempt at the same time to describe the contemporary ecumenical horizon within which contemporary theology is being done. The introduction sketches the post-World War II background of contemporary Protestant, Catholic and Jewish theology. Each of the nine studies focuses on a representative of a particular theological trend. The conclusion is an attempt to project the basic task of Christian and Jewish theology in the last quarter of the twentieth century. The focus here is primarily on Christian theology and its primary function in relation to ministry. The basic problem of any introduction to theology today is that of aiming, not simply at a moving target but at one that seems to be moving in all directions at once. This book deals with theologians whose works are likely to set the pace for years to come, but that amounts to a calculated guess on the part of the editor. In any case it should serve as background for any new trends that might appear in the near future.

The occasion for conceiving and trying out experimentally these ecumenical studies as an introduction to theology was a course for the Adult Ecumenical Education Program of Nutley, New Jersey. Several Protestant churches joined the Roman Catholic parishes and the Jewish synagogue in sponsoring this experimental program. More than 180 people registered. Since the course was taught, The Nutley Ecumenical Council has been formed to promote adult ecumenical education in the community of Nutley. The royalties of this book are dedicated to The Nutley Ecumenical Council as long as it exists in a form that promotes ecumenical education.

The people who deserve special mention for the help and encouragement they provided for the development of these studies are too many for me to name them all. I wish to thank the team of discussion leaders who took extra training to be able to perform their task in the small groups. But three people must be mentioned as those without whom the course would never have happened. The Reverend David Follansbee of Vincent Methodist Church dreamed the dream in the first place. Mr. J. C. Brown and Mr. Frank Januzzi served as co-chairmen, teachers, ambassadors between the churches and the synagogue, organizers, and general servants for the whole enterprise. What they accomplished and the manner in which it was carried out in their retirement years have given the rest of us much to live up to. In the challenge of their example they have given many something to look forward to.

I wish to thank Ms. Sharon Flynn for her help in preparation of the original studies. She proved to be as much a theological consultant as a typist and proof reader. Finally, I want to thank those students of The Theological School at Drew University who in my classes have insisted that the language of instruction be American English and not the jargon that theologians use with each other. It has been impossible to eliminate all traces of it from these studies, but the goal has been to bridge the gap between theologese and English.

Michael D. Ryan

Drew Forest
Eastertide, 1974

INTRODUCTION AND BACKGROUND

The Crisis of Faith Between the Times

Our present civilization is preoccupied with the problem of change. Like a man who looks into a mirror and suddenly realizes "I'm old," many of our institutions--political, economic, and ecclesiastical--are feeling their age. They are painfully aware of the pressure of vital forces and new institutions around them demanding that they change, that they adapt to new conditions of life. With this kind of pressure often comes a nostalgia for the relative simplicity of a century ago. It results in the temptation to carry on the basic enterprise of the institution as if the new forces do not really exist, or are, at most, peripheral matters that do not have to be taken seriously. In some instances the leadership deems it a positive duty to resist all pressures for fundamental change for the sake of preserving the traditional integrity of the institution. In such cases change is viewed as betrayal and is accompanied by guilt feelings when it does occur.

Another equally unrealistic attitude can also be found in the very same institutions, namely, the assumption that any change is to be preferred to a given status quo. Accordingly, any and all resistance to change, any questions raised as to the propriety of proposed changes, are viewed as self-serving and evil. Here, every failure to change becomes an occasion for institutional self-recrimination.

The best interests of any basic institution of society cannot be served by either of these extreme attitudes--the one to resist all change, the other to promote change at all costs. They do not lend themselves to the sober appraisal of the institution and its situation in the world which authentic change or authentic resistance to change might require. It would seem that in the long run both of these attitudes end up as victims of change--the former because change happens in spite of all resistance, and the latter because no resistance

1

has been applied for the purpose of focusing and directing all efforts at change toward a greater good, or at least toward a lesser evil. The sad fact of our day is that these extreme, unhealthy attitudes toward change are polarizing almost every institution in our society and thus inhibiting healthy development. The Congress of the United States, the General Assembly of the United Nations, and almost every religious body in the world exhibit such polarizing tendencies. Why is this?

One is tempted to answer this question with the bland observation that our century is a time of transition, but that would amount to a gross understatement. Every age is a time of transition in so far as life brings with it change and development. Scientific and cultural observers are saying that what makes our time unprecedented in history is the speed and the amount of change in our society. The nearest analogy that some can find is the discovery of fire, or the development of agriculture which made civilization possible in the first place. Modern technology is seen as transforming both the social fabric and the structures of civilization itself. The pressure resulting from such pervasive change has produced the extreme responses that we find in every institution.

Alvin Toffler, in his book, Future Shock, gave a name to the cultural illness that results from such rampant, burgeoning change. He explored the physical and the psychological effects of the mercurial transformation in the twentieth century from a society oriented towards permanence to a society oriented towards transience in the products and relationships of its people. Toffler sought to demonstrate from current data that the new society of transience has not ended up, as many feared it might, in a rigid standardization and leveling of life. Instead, it produced a condition which he called "overchoice" for all of its members.

What Toffler himself did not discern was that this condition of overchoice would itself prove to be most transitory. His data refuting standardization appeared at the zenith of technological over-development, but standardization and leveling of life may yet appear as part of a process of de-development that is just now getting started. Toffler's own example, the variety offered car buyers as to models and equipment, seems to be in the first phase of a radical reduction after the 1973-74 fuel shortage. The cover of Newsweek for April 1, 1974 bears the title "Detroit Thinks Small" next to a portrait of Henry Ford II. The awareness that technologized industry has been gobbling up natural resources with amazing rapidity has created a new "future shock." The prospect of rapid de-development due to demands outrunning supply in such essentials as fuel and water has dawned on the American consciousness. How shall we cope with a transience that will move from affluence to poverty in a future characterized by shortages and social disorganization? This question discloses the religious dimension of our current future shock. Basically, it is a crisis of faith.

Hermann Hesse gave expression to the contemporary crisis of faith as long ago as 1927 in his novel Steppenwolf. Harry Haller, the lone genius of the novel, put it this way:

> A man of the Middle Ages would detest the whole mode of our present-day life as something far more than horrible, far more than barbarous. Every age, every culture, every custom and tradition has its own character, its own weakness and its own strength, its beauties and ugliness; accepts certain sufferings as matters of course, puts up patiently with certain evils. Human life is reduced to real suffering, to hell, only when two ages, two cultures and religions overlap. A man of the Classical Age who had to live in medieval times would suffocate miserably just as a savage does in the midst of our civilization. Now there are times when a whole generation is caught in this way between two ages, two modes of life, with the consequence that it loses all power to understand itself and has no standard, no security, no simple acquiescence. Naturally everyone does not feel this equally strongly. A nature such as Nietzsche's had to suffer our present ills more than a generation in advance. What he had to go through alone and misunderstood, thousands suffer today.[1]

The hell of being caught between two ages is abysmally greater in our day. The civilization and religion of permanence and the civilization and religion of transience are pulling in opposite directions, tearing the souls of men asunder. The religion of permanence focuses on the eternal, immutable character of its God and lays great stress on the unity of form for the expression of the unity of faith in creeds and rites. The religion of transience speaks of the vital, dynamic character of its God in terms of a divine "Becoming." The evidence of the vitality of religion is here seen in the multiplicity of forms emerging from the dynamic process of life

itself. Here, unity is discerned not in forms but in the life
that creates them. The religion of transience brings with its
many forms, not a single theology but many. It appears in
our time as an explosion of theology, a surfeit of theological
options as new disciplines such as ecology and thanatology
(the study of death) provide new perspectives on the manifold
character of religious life. Today a theologian may follow
one methodology or a combination drawn from a number of
disciplines, including sociology, psychology, history, philosophy, literature, and anthropology. The result, as a perusal
of any number of current theological journals readily reveals,
is the spectacle of theology literally taking off in all directions
at once. The primary question for many today is, "What is
the meaning of this multiplicity of theologies?" For others it
is, "Can a unity nevertheless be discerned in this multiplicity?"
From the writings offered for study and reflection in this volume it should be clear that contemporary theology is grappling
with these questions and is seeking to respond appropriately to
the epochal changes of our time.

The Community of Faith, Theology, and Change

World War II has proved to be a kind of historical wa-
tershed for the community of faith, whether Protestant, Catholic or Jewish. When in the summer of 1948 the First Assembly of the World Council of Churches met in Amsterdam, the
battle-scarred landscape and the ruins of bombed-out buildings
revivified the sights and sounds of war in the minds of many
of the delegates, especially of Americans who were seeing it
for the first time. Instead of the dove of peace, the linger-
ing spectre of war cast its shadow over the assembly of main-
ly Protestant clergymen. The vast devastation of Europe suggested to many the end of an era. The historical horizon extended from World War II back to World War I, and war
clouds seemed to darken the horizon of the future. It was not
a moment for soaring optimism. Reinhold Niebuhr spoke for
many when he said in his address, "We are witnessing, and
participating in, the decline of European civilization...."[2]
Niebuhr went on to say that the recent conflagration spelled
the end of the dream of a Christian civilization. The idea of
a Christo-morphic society, of institutions conformed to the
image of Christ, was over. For this new, bleak moment of
western history Niebuhr offered as a resource the thinking
that he had developed most cogently in his work, The Nature
and the Destiny of Man. Christians should not expect a final
solution to sin and to social evil within history. Henceforth,

Christians should work for peace and justice in an alien society that could scarcely be less interested in their basic
motive--namely, the gospel of the love of God revealed
through Jesus Christ as the forgiveness of sins. In Niebuhr's
forecast Christianity itself would be more or less anonymous
in the post-war world. Christians would have their own resources for social and political involvement in a secularized
civilization. Niebuhr exhorted the Assembly as follows:

> We ought as Christians to strive more, and not
> less, earnestly for the peace of nations. We ought
> not to be indifferent to the problem of what techni-
> cal-political instruments are best suited to maintain
> a tolerable peace and to express man's obligation to
> his neighbour. On the other hand our faith ought to
> supply us with a resource which secular idealism
> lacks. We must learn to do our duty in the peace
> of our security in God, which is not disturbed by
> the alternate furies of unjustified hopes and unjusti-
> fied despair. Knowing that 'neither life nor death
> ... can separate us from the love of God which is
> in Christ Jesus our Lord' we will not be surprised
> to discover that all historic securities are imper-
> fect. [3]

For the Jewish community World War II in its terrible
political aspects was but a crude facade covering a chasm of
distilled evil with a sign on it, "For Jews Only." Two out
of every five European Jews were shoved into that chasm as
some six million human beings were efficiently exterminated
and incinerated by the Nazi technology of death. The "Holocaust," as it is now called, has become a new event for many
believing Jews in the covenantal history of Israel. As the division of the kingdom after Solomon, or the Babylonian captiv-
ity of the Jews, so also the Holocaust was at once a political
and a religious event calling for a decision of faith. Because
it was also the latter, the covenant faith of Israel was either
renewed in, or ruthlessly rooted out of, the hearts of those
who understood themselves as witnesses to the decimation of
their own people. Thus the Holocaust has resulted in the religious polarization of the Jewish community. Elie Wiesel
and Emil Fackenheim bear witness to the renewal of the covenant through the fires of the Holocaust. Richard Rubenstein
sees in it the end of what he calls "the pathetic delusion of
my people. "[4]

But strangely, in spite of this religious polarization,

the Holocaust has also had a unifying effect on Jews as a people in history. Whether their faith in the covenant was renewed, or whether that faith went up with the smoke of their loved ones, many Jews, especially those who today live in Israel, cannot express their identity as a people apart from the event of the Holocaust. They live in the post-European-Christian civilization of our time as the people of the Holocaust. Their presence is at once a reminder of the terrible hatred that produced the death camps, and a prophetic call to repent of all self-consuming, world-destroying, person-eradicating HATE.

For this people the Holocaust is a unique event qualifying the whole history that led to it. They see no way back to the past except by way of the interpretation of the Holocaust, and no other way into the future. They are challenging the Christian Church as an institution, and individual Christians as well, to look at their own history in the light of the Holocaust. Can a Christian honestly study the history of Christian hatred for Jews and not be horrified by the Christian precedents for the death camps?[5] If the relation of Christianity and Judaism is a matter of great concern to the Church, as it surely ought to be, there is no other way to realize it except by the self-understanding that Christianity will develop in facing up to the Holocaust. The questions which the very presence of the people of the Holocaust raises for Christianity is, "Can there be any genuine renewal of Christianity apart from a radical self-examination in the light of the Holocaust?"

The historical facts of Christian hatred and persecution of Jews were known and well documented before World War II by Jewish and Christian scholars. H. Graetz's Popular History of the Jews (New York: Jordan Publishing Co., 1935) has been a representative Jewish interpretation, and James W. Parkes' work, The Conflict of the Church and the Synagogue (first published in 1934 and later as a Meridian Paperback in 1961) presented an honest assessment by a Christian historian. Under the shocking impact of the Holocaust the ground has been covered again by many scholars in an attempt to understand the historical roots of the death camps. Noteworthy works are Leon Poliakov's The History of Anti-Semitism (New York: Vanguard Press, 1965) and Edward Flannery's The Anguish of the Jews: Twenty Three Centuries of Anti-Semitism (New York: Macmillan Paperback, 1965), which tells the story from a Roman Catholic perspective. Some recent works have gone beyond the recitation of the facts of persecution and Christian expressions of hatred for Jews and have begun to examine the dogmatic structures of Christian theology in the light of these facts. Robert L. Wilken's work, Judaism and The Early Christian Mind (New Haven: Yale University Press, 1971) scrutinizes the exegesis and theology of Cyril of Alexandria and ably demonstrates the role of anti-Judaism in the theological enterprise of that fifth-century church father. Alan T. Davies' Anti-Semitism and the Christian Mind: The Crisis of Conscience after Auschwitz (New York: Herder & Herder, 1969) presents an excellent survey of recent Jewish and Christian writings responding to the Holocaust along with his own delineation of the theological and moral issues which Christian anti-Semitism poses for the Christian church. This work takes an important step in the direction of a full-blown Christian death camp theology, but as yet such a work has not been written. [6]

Twenty years after World War II the Phoenix flew. A new civilization appeared on the soil of old Europe. More accurately, two civilizations appeared. One is communist and dominated by Russia and the other is capitalist and dominated by the United States. On the surface the new capitalist civilization still showed many evidences of its Christian heritage. In great cities like Konrad Adenauer's Cologne, the beautiful cathedral still stood out above the new modern buildings all around it. The name "Christian" even appeared in a couple of the new political parties of Germany. But it was obvious to everyone that these parties did not really represent the Christian Church. They represented the new Germany committed to technological advance and economic success in the world market, just as most political parties of the several nations of Europe were doing for their own countries. The result was the swift transformation of European life. Those who had an eye for the source of most of the technological change, whether as to conception or capital finances, referred to it as "the Americanization of Europe."

In the context of this new civilization transforming the continent of Europe, Pope John XXIII called The Second Vatican Council of the Roman Catholic Church, which met from October, 1962 to November, 1965. In the documents of Vatican II are to be found the official responses of the Roman Catholic Church to the events of the new era: to the post-war developments in European society, to other Christian bodies, to Jews, to other world religions, to humanism, to atheism, to change itself. In "The Pastoral Constitution on the Church in the Modern World," promulgated by Pope Paul

VI on December 7, 1965, the following statement appeared:

> The living conditions of modern man have been so
> profoundly changed in their social and cultural di-
> mensions, that we can speak of a new age in hu-
> man history. [7]

There is no question but that the authors of this Pastoral Constitution saw technology as the single greatest force
"transforming the face of the earth" and also as "already trying to master outer space."[8] But it is equally true that they
did not claim to understand all of the tremendous implications
of this force. They gave expression to the overwhelming impact of the new technological age as follows:

> History itself speeds along on so rapid a course that
> an individual person can scarcely keep abreast of it.
> The destiny of the human community has become all
> of a piece, where once the various groups of men
> had a kind of private history of their own. Thus,
> the human race has passed from a rather static
> concept of reality to a more dynamic evolutionary
> one. In consequence, there has arisen a new ser-
> ies of problems, a series as important as can be,
> calling for new efforts of analysis and synthesis.[9]
> (Italics added)

Having declared that whole new way of conceiving reality had
accompanied the transformation of civilization, the fathers of
Vatican II, quite appropriately and quite in keeping with their
modesty, called for rigorous new investigations on the part
of Churchmen so that they might better understand the new
realities confronting them in the modern world. Far from
being left out of this enterprise, theologians were called to
think through the implications of new knowledge for the Christian faith:

> These difficulties do not necessarily harm the life
> of faith. Indeed they can stimulate the mind to a
> more accurate and penetrating grasp of the faith.
> For recent studies and findings of science, history
> and philosophy raise new questions which influence
> life and demand new theological investigations.
>
> Furthermore, while adhering to the methods and
> requirements proper to theology, theologians are
> invited to seek continually for more suitable ways

of communicating doctrine to the men of their times. For the deposit of faith or revealed truths are one thing; the manner in which they are formulated without violence to their meaning and significance is another.

In pastoral care, appropriate use must be made not only of theological principles, but also of the findings of the secular sciences, especially of psychology and sociology. Thus the faithful can be brought to live the faith in a more thorough and mature way.[10]

The paragraphs just cited constitute the mandate from Vatican II that lay behind that much used and abused word, "aggiornamento" or "up-dating." The popular press reporting on the Council either misunderstood or ignored the very serious attempt to distinguish between "the deposit of faith," as the essence of the Christian faith in linguistic form is called by Roman Catholics, and the statements which express that faith for a particular time and place after the time of the Apostles. The world was given the weird impression that Catholic theologians were authorized to change the faith received from the Apostles. Indeed, a few radicals attempted to capitalize on this misunderstanding by encouraging laymen to take positions that would place them outside of their own historical community of faith. The work of these radicals has been mischievous, for it has produced a reaction within the Roman Catholic community against up-dating in the authorized sense of finding a contemporary way of expressing the traditional faith.

Professor James Hitchcock, a historian at St. Louis University, in a recent book called The Decline and Fall of Radical Catholicism (Herder & Herder, 1971), charged that aggiornamento has been a failure because it has led to a widespread denial of the faith.[11] By focusing on radical thinkers from both Protestant and Catholic circles, Professor Hitchcock himself undermined authentic ecumenism by treating ecumenical thinking as a cover for unbelief. It is also quite possible that he has recognized and is recoiling from the very real risk involved when the traditional Christian faith is critically examined for the purpose of finding a way to communicate it. But in spite of the radicals who received just criticism from Hitchcock, neither aggiornamento nor ecumenism has been a failure. Both together have unleashed a scholarly productivity and creativity among Catholic theologians that have amounted to a veritable renaissance of Catholic theology in a single decade. The Christian theologians to be reckoned with today are Roman Catholic. Men like Karl Rahner, Bernard Lonergan, Hans Küng and Edward Schillebeeckx are playing the role of Karl Barth, Rudolf Bultmann, Emil Brunner and Paul Tillich for this generation. The works of these men and of those who either have defended them or opposed them in genuine, calm, scholarly debate have constituted the beginning of a new epoch in the history of theology, and with it has come a whole new possibility for dialogue among all Christians, Jews, and genuine seekers after truth in the world, no matter what their religious persuasion happens to be.

The Contemporary Explosion of Theology

As the passages cited above from the "Pastoral Constitution on the Church in the Modern World" readily acknowledged, new studies and findings in science and history have raised new questions for theology. [12] So have recent studies in relatively newer disciplines such as anthropology and ecology. This accumulation of new knowledge, plus the great unsolved problems of mankind: war, hunger, poverty, racism, religious bigotry, plus the rise of a new technological civilization, plus the vitality of other world religions--all these factors fed into theology, be it Christian or Jewish, have led to the contemporary explosion. The result has been many new directions in theological thinking which have cut across denominational and confessional lines. We shall examine a few of the more significant of these directions in this volume, but first let us attempt to assess the situation of an exploding theology. Three aspects of the explosion are important matters to be examined for any grasp of this complex situation.

First, let us not be surprised that the crisis of faith in our time and the explosion of theology have produced some casualties, and that the casualties should be theologians themselves. Theology itself has always been a risk. To speak of the things of God, the Holy, before men is nothing if not foolish. Theologians are those who have been willing to take this risk. It should not surprise us then that the kind of person who would become a theologian should be willing to say unpleasant, unpopular things with great courage--even if the unpleasant, unpopular thing is that he can no longer believe what he once believed. Dr. Van A. Harvey of the University of Pennsylvania described these qualities very well in a recent

essay called "The Alienated Theologian."[13] Wherever serious
questing after truth takes place in the name of faith there is
the possibility that the faith itself will be questioned and rejected. That is the inherent danger which has always accompanied theology. It is, so to speak, a professional hazard,
and one which has always been recognized by laymen, too,
who for this reason tend to be suspicious of theologians. But
it is also possible that the faith will be questioned and embraced on a deeper, more profound level. That is the serious possibility that motivates the genuine theologians of Catholic renewal, for example, both Karl Rahner and Hans Küng,
no matter what they might say about each other. While the
temptation is there for those who have rejected the faith and
those who have embraced the faith to condemn one another in
unfortunate ad hominem statements, those who have once believed and who have seriously questioned their faith have a
great sympathy and understanding for one another in spite of
their radically different results. Unbelief continues to haunt
the believing theologian, and faith haunts the unbeliever.
Both know it, for both have been there. That is why they
avidly read one another's books. The day that they stop doing that is the day that they give up the serious quest for
truth.

Second, exploding theology means a plurality of theol-
ogies--even within one community of faith. In a certain sense,
this has always been true in so far as every community has
its historical legacy of different theologies. But now theologians, especially Christian theologians, are questioning whether a comprehensive systematic statement of the Christian
faith for our time is possible at all. The statement of faith
is now being made in more concrete terms, speaking to "all
sorts and conditions of men," but not to all of them at once.
Karl Rahner put it this way in his book, The Christian of the
Future:

> ... genuine 'progress' in dogmatic development in
> the future will move, not so much in the direction
> of a wider, more exact unfolding and precise defi-
> nition of traditional dogma, but simply in that of a
> more living, radical grasp and statement of the ul-
> timate fundamental dogmas themselves. A unified,
> universally valid statement of this kind could be
> accompanied by quite a number of theologies jux-
> taposed in a pluralist way, not contradicting each
> other of course, but not susceptible of being posi-
> tively incorporated into a higher synthesis. In

short, it is conceivable that the 'change' in the
Church's teaching on dogma and morals may move
in the direction of quite considerable 'decontrol'
and a general tendency to leave questions open.
That does not mean leaving people to do what they
like, but imposes a greater burden of responsibility
on the individual. [14]

In his recent work, Contours of Faith, John Dillenberger, a Protestant theologian, addressed himself to the same
problem from his perspective. Having stated his opinion early in the book that Paul Tillich may represent "the last of the
great systems,"[15] Dillenberger later went on to say:

A new diversity is entering into theological work.
Within the theological community no one can any
longer be equally at home in all the facets of theology, much less the systematic discipline the theologian once thought he must unify. While a vision of
the whole may be a human longing, no one can any
longer create a unified system of any major significance. Theology will demand teamwork or the
sharing of theological labors, where scholars learn
from one another and gladly accept the enriching
fruits of the labours of others. [16]

The fact of this multiplicity of theologies and the
teamwork which has already begun suggest that theology will
remain ecumenical in character in spite of all the detractors
of ecumenism and in spite of the many ill-advised enterprises that have been undertaken in its name. From a Roman
Catholic perspective one would have to erase Vatican II and
its documents from the historical record in order to eliminate ecumenism. From a Protestant perspective ecumenism
will take on a new meaning once the significance of Vatican
II has been appropriated. It means that the old style "Protestant" ecumenism, of attempting to find a single, common-
denominator type of theology and a single institutional expression for the Christian faith, will be replaced by the more
"Catholic" and more spiritual ecumenism of Vatican II, which
is willing to carry on deep dialogue about the faith across
theological and institutional differences without an agenda for
institutional unification. Catholic ecumenism recognizes that
these differences can never be dissolved by discussion, but
rather that they can be the occasion for acknowledging sins
committed against other communities of faith and thus open
the way to a unity that will consist, at the very least, of a

consciousness of a shared history and of a shared present time and place for the service of God.

It is most significant that the Roman Catholic Church, with its historic emphasis on unity of form, should through its leaders and theologians be pointing practically to a unity in diversity at this juncture in history. The stance is most realistic, giving ecumenism a new impulse just when Protestant ecumenism is exhausted. The following excerpts from the Decree on Ecumenism of Vatican II express the basis and the character of what I have called "Catholic" ecumenism:

> 7. There can be no ecumenism worthy of the name without a change of heart. For it is from newness of attitudes (cf. Eph. 4:23), from self-denial and unstinted love, that yearnings for unity take their rise and grow toward maturity....
>
> St. John has testified: 'If we say that we have not sinned, we make him a liar, and his word is not in us' (I Jn. 1:10). This holds good for sins against unity. Thus, in humble prayer, we beg pardon of God and of our separated brethren, just as we forgive those who trespass against us....
>
> 8. This change of heart and holiness of life, along with public and private prayer for the unity of Christians, should be regarded as the soul of the whole ecumenical movement, and can rightly be called 'spiritual ecumenism.' ...
>
> 10. Instruction in sacred theology and other branches of knowledge, especially those of a historical nature, must also be presented from an ecumenical point of view, so that at every point they may more accurately correspond with the facts of the case....
>
> 11. The manner and order in which Catholic belief is expressed should in no way become an obstacle to dialogue with our brethren. It is, of course, essential that doctrine be clearly presented in its entirety. Nothing is so foreign to the spirit of ecumenism as a false conciliatory approach which harms the purity of Catholic doctrine and obscures its assured genuine meaning. [17]

Such ecumenism clearly does not expect the Roman Catholic

Church to forsake its own heritage in the name of a new superficial unity, nor does it expect that those Christian communities designated as the "separated brethren" will simply
forsake their particular heritage of faith. It does expect that
all Christian communions would search "together ... into the
divine mysteries," and that they "should act with love for
truth, with charity, and with humility."[18] Thus, it is at
base an ecumenism of study, of education and of action,
where such action bespeaks a unity of faith beyond all of the
historic differences.

Third, Christian theologians are in the process of
coming to terms with their task of helping their Churches:
their leadership and their laity, to understand the minority
status of Christianity in virtually every society in the world
today. Karl Rahner projected as a future situation back in
1965 what is apparently becoming more and more real with
each passing year. Speaking of the Christian or Catholic
communities of the future, he said:

> Everywhere they will be a little flock, because man-
> kind grows quicker than Christendom and because
> men will not be Christians by custom and tradition,
> through institutions and history, or because of the
> homogeneity of a social milieu and public opinion,
> but leaving out of account the sacred flame of pa-
> rental example and the intimate sphere of home,
> family or small groups--they will be Christians on-
> ly because of their own act of faith attained in a
> difficult struggle and perpetually achieved anew.
> Everywhere will be diaspora and the diaspora will
> be everywhere....
>
> Nowhere will there be any more 'Catholic nations'
> which put a Christian stamp on men prior to any
> personal decision.[19]

What Hendrick Kraemer said back in 1938 with his
book, The Christian Message in a Non-Christian World, is
only now really beginning to sink into the consciousness of
American churches as more and more evidence of their minority status as "Christian" communities accumulates. The
strategies for "winning the nation to Christ" will very soon be
replaced by strategies for the survival of the Christian witness to and in all nations. The latter strategies will have a
quite different expectation with regard to statistics than the
former. This shift in basic strategy for a minority Church

will require more theological acumen on the part of the whole Church, such as would be nurtured by historical investigations into the early Church's struggle for survival. Laymen will have to participate in these studies since they will play the crucial role in the new strategy, as clergy did in the strategies of the majority Church.

It is precisely with respect to the strategy of survival that the dialogue between Christians and Jews will be most important. While there is little reason to expect that Jews, especially the survivors of the Holocaust, would even want to share the accumulated wisdom of their people on this matter and on what it means to live in diaspora, surely Christians would be well advised to study Jewish documents and Jewish history for such wisdom. In the course of living in their own diaspora, Christians might for the first time really understand what it means to be a Jew in America. As Christians demonstrate their knowledge of Jewish tradition, dialogue will become more natural and free flowing. But Christians will have to have endured the pain of discovering that Israel was forced to develop a strategy for survival largely in the face of Christian persecutions.

In his work, Legends of Our Time, Elie Wiesel tells the story of a Spaniard of Saragossa who discovered that he was Jewish only when he finally met a Jew who could read a parchment handed down for generations in his family as an amulet. The Spaniard was perplexed and angry at this revelation, not so much because he was indeed Jewish, but because he had been conditioned by his society and culture to think that Jews did not really exist. The document, which was written in the time of the Spanish Catholic persecution of the Jews at the end of the fifteenth century, read as follows:

> I, Moses, son of Abraham, forced to break all ties with my people and my faith, leave these lines to the children of my children and to theirs, in order that on the day when Israel will be able to walk again, its head high under the sun, without fear and without remorse, they will know where their roots lie. Written at Saragossa, this ninth day of the month of Av, in the year of punishment and exile. [20]

Whether Christians will ever have to employ such a strategy for survival remains an open question. It is not likely in the near future, but the Nazi terror proved that it could happen once again in the twentieth century for Jews. There are forces at work in the world which could, if they were to secure a monopoly of political power, direct such terror toward Christians. The question before us is whether the rather flaccid Christianity of America has any survival capacity at all, since it has enjoyed public acceptance and toleration from the time of the birth of the nation. Probably the first test for American Christians and for American Jews, too, is whether their faith can survive the contemporary explosion of theology and the new diaspora condition which has appeared on the scene.

NOTES

1. Hermann Hesse, Steppenwolf, translated by Basil Creighton (New York, Chicago, San Francisco: Holt, Rinehart & Winston, Inc., 1957, 1961), p. 22f. Used by permission of the publisher.

2. Reinhold Niebuhr, "God's Design and the Present Disorder of Civilization," The Church and the Disorder of Society, Vol. III, The Amsterdam Assembly Series (New York: Harper & Bros., 1948), p. 16. Used by permission.

3. Ibid., p. 26.

4. For the dramatic difference between Emil Fackenheim's and Richard Rubenstein's responses to the Holocaust, see: E. Fackenheim, "The People Israel Lives!" The Christian Century, May 6, 1970, pp. 563-568, and R. Rubenstein, "God as Cosmic Sadist," The Christian Century, July 29, 1970, pp. 921-923.

5. See Richard Rubenstein's essay, "Religion and the Origins of the Death Camps" in After Auschwitz (New York: Bobbs-Merrill, 1966), pp. 1-46; also Robert L. Wilken, "Insignissima Religio, Certe Licita? Christianity and Judaism in the Fourth and Fifth Centuries," in Jerald C. Brauer, ed., The Impact of the Church Upon Its Culture (Chicago: University of Chicago Press, 1968), pp. 39-66.

6. The selections from Hans Küng's The Church included below in Study Two in the section entitled "The Church and the Jews," pp. 47-51, are indicative of the importance that Küng places upon the history of

the relations between the Church and Judaism in his theological work.

7. Walter M. Abbott, ed., "Pastoral Constitution on the Church in the Modern World, " Documents of Vatican II (New York: America Press, 1966), p. 260. This and following extended quotations used by permission of the publisher. All rights reserved. © 1966, America Press, Inc.

8. Ibid., p. 203.

9. Ibid., p. 203f.

10. Ibid., p. 268f.

11. An excerpt of the book was published in Commonweal, May 14, 1971, under the title, "Aggiornamento has Failed, " pp. 231-234.

12. See above note 10.

13. Van A. Harvey, "The Alienated Theologian, " found in The Future of Philosophical Theology, ed. Robert A. Evans (Philadelphia: Westminster Press, 1971), pp. 113-142.

14. Karl Rahner, The Christian of the Future (New York: Herder & Herder, 1967), p. 34. Used by permission of the publisher.

15. John Dillenberger, Contours of Faith (Nashville: Abingdon Press, 1969), p. 59. Used by permission of the publisher. © Abingdon Press, 1969.

16. Ibid., p. 155.

17. "The Decree on Ecumenism, " The Documents of Vatican II, pp. 351-354, edited. Reprinted by permission of the publisher. All rights reserved.

18. Ibid., p. 354.

19. Karl Rahner, "The Future Reality of Christian Life, " The Christian of the Future (New York: Herder & Herder, 1967), p. 79. Reprinted by permission of the publisher.

20. Elie Wiesel, "Testament of a Jew in Saragossa," Legends of Our Time, (New York: Holt, Rinehart & Winston, Inc., 1968), p. 67. Reprinted by permission of the publisher.

Part I

THEOLOGY IN CRISIS

Study 1

LANGDON GILKEY

THE CRISIS OF THE WORD "GOD"

A Prophetic Theologian

It was probably accidental that one of the relatively
few American civilians who spent most of World War II in a
Japanese internment camp should later have become one of
America's foremost Protestant theologians.   Or was it accidental?   Gilkey returned from his experience as one who had
witnessed the essence of humanity squeezed out of some fine,
upstanding American citizens by the pressures of life in a
crowded compound in Shantung province, China.   He also returned a committed Christian.   On the surface the contrast
between the small, tight world of the internment camp in Asia
and the vast, open expanse of life in affluent America could
hardly have been greater.   This contrast registered itself in
Gilkey's consciousness with overwhelming force, but even
more strange to him was the dramatic continuity between
human life in the camp and human life in the continental
United States in the late nineteen forties.   Gilkey appeared
to friends and acquaintances, to Church and civic groups as
a young man who had returned from another world, but who
strangely insisted that that other world was not very different from our own United States.   A touch of the prophet
rested with Gilkey then, and has never really left him.

Gilkey was a teacher of English and philosophy at
Yenching University in the city of Peking during the first
part of World War II.   In March of 1943 he was part of a
group of some four hundred Americans, including very young
children and aged men and women, who were marched through
the streets of the city in full view of a Chinese throng assembled by the Japanese to witness the humiliation of the
white westerners.   The Americans lurched and staggered
under their loads; they had been permitted to keep only what
they could carry to the internment camp.   In his memoir

called Shantung Compound, Gilkey wrote, "... the era of Western dominance in Asia ended with that burdened crawl to the station. "[1]

The journey to the compound near Weihsien was a foretaste of the next two and a half years. The Americans were crowded into small railroad cars with wooden benches for seats. They had very little food and water for a journey that was to last all night and most of the next day. At the camp they again experienced unbelievable congestion as two thousand people were jammed into a space of less than a city block. It was a prison with machine guns constantly trained on them, but in spite of the lack of food and heat, and the unsanitary conditions, Gilkey found no cause to accuse his Japanese captors of maltreatment. The great ordeal of the camp was to learn to live with other Americans under the conditions of extreme privation. Gilkey gained two basic insights at Weihsien that have lent continuity to his subsequent theological development:

> First, it seemed certain enough that man is immensely creative, ingenious, and courageous in the face of new problems. But it was also equally apparent that under pressure he loves himself and his own more than he will ever admit. Furthermore, both the universality and yet the puzzling 'unnaturalness' of this self-love were certainly established by our experience, for men consistently denied the motivations which equally consistently determined their conduct. If men were just plain 'good' this self-love would not have been so clearly pervasive in all they did. If, on the other hand, they were just plain 'bad, ' if this self-love were simply 'natural' to man, those who acted upon it would not have been so intent to deny its presence and to claim that their acts flowed from moral intentions. [2]

The other insight was:

> The only hope in the human situation is that the 're-ligiousness' of men find its true center in God, and not in the many idols that appear in the course of our experience. If men are to forget themselves enough to share with each other, to be honest under pressure, and to be rational and moral enough to establish community, they must have some center of loyalty and devotion, some source of security and

meaning, beyond their own welfare. [3]

By 1963, Gilkey joined the faculty of the Divinity School of The University of Chicago, after having taught a number of years in the Divinity School at Vanderbilt University. Though a strong strain of Paul Tillich's thinking could, and still can, be detected in his theology, Gilkey combined it with an appreciation of the history of Protestantism in America which enabled him to speak to the American situation much more directly than could Tillich. This Gilkey did in his book, How the Church Can Minister to the World Without Losing Itself. In view of his most recent theological writings, it is possible that Gilkey might now consider the theological posture of that book as dated. Nevertheless, it remains a trenchant criticism of Protestant denominations in twentieth-century America.

In that work Gilkey was concerned with what might be called the eclipse of the Holy, of the truly Sacred, in modern Protestant denominations. He asked:

> Is there in American Protestantism a living and real transcendence? Is there any sense of a transcendent Word that enlightens and forms the church and its life, any real sense of the presence of God in worship, of a transcendent standard by which the church measures its own ethical life and the behavior of its people? Is there any real element of the holy in our contemporary churches? [4]

With a penetrating analytical eye, Gilkey laid bare the genuine crisis of the modern Protestant denominations as a crisis of "the Word of God." He went on to describe the particular present conditions of the current famine of the word of God in these bodies. American Protestant denominations derive, in his view, from post-reformation sectarian Christianity. [5] Employing Ernst Troeltsch's distinction between "church-type" and "sect-type" religious communities, [6] Gilkey argued that sects like the Anabaptists, the Quakers and the Baptists and the American Campbellites were originally just as opposed to the world as the more traditional churches such as the Roman Catholic, the Lutheran and the Church of England, but the two types of community expressed their opposition in a different way.

These "church-type" religious communities were made up of people who were very much involved in the affairs of

their world and so made many personal compromises of their
Christian convictions in the course of living in the world. [7]
But at the center of these communities were sacred elements
which were never submitted to the world's judgment and which
guaranteed for the whole community a sense of the Holy.
They consisted of such things as: the holy offices in Catholicism, sacraments, dogmas, the Word as pure doctrine in
Lutheranism, etc. In these sacred matters the world was
not permitted to have a say. The sect type of community
rejected the idea of sacred elements, and especially the idea
of the clergy as having a special power of authority that is
not available to laymen. The preachers of the sects came
from the ranks of the people as spokesmen among equals.
The Holy was not for them something objective in the sense
that it could be handled by men. It was rather subjective in
the sense that it was a personal experience for everyone
whose eyes had been enlightened by the Holy Spirit to understand the Bible. But far from capitulating to the world around
them, the sect-type communities maintained many of the attitudes toward the world that characterized the monastic communities of the Middle Ages. They refused to participate in
the political institutions of society, to fight in war, to study
the worldly disciplines of philosophy, science, literature, and
they refrained from attending the world's amusements. The
sects maintained an otherness to the world, even as they
lived in it.

The American denomination is, according to Gilkey, a
new form of religious community which combines aspects of
the other two. Like the older church-type community, its
members are very much involved in the world and its institutions. They study in its universities, read its literature,
attend its amusements and sports events. But in terms of
institutional polity, the denomination is sectarian in character. It tends to emphasize individual experience and personal religion more than doctrine and theology. Laymen control
the purse strings and with that, a great deal of the day-to-
day operations of the denomination. Denominational ministers
are not considered as priests so much as representative persons who are examples of the faith, or spokesmen for the
community of faith about the faith. "Here, then, " Gilkey
concluded, "we have in the denomination the sect-type in
Christendom, in culture. "[8] What has happened with this development is that there is no distinct or profound sense of
the Holy to be discerned in it. What has always been peculiar to the Church is here "in fact in imminent danger of being
engulfed by the world. "[9]

Within a year after the publication of <u>How the Church</u> <u>Can Minister</u> ... Gilkey found himself in a radically altered theological situation. Until that time he understood himself as speaking to a Church that was suffering a famine "of hearing the words of the Lord."[10] He saw his task as that of reminding the Church of her divine calling through the transcendent Word of God. It was prophetic, neo-orthodox theology and its purpose was to call a fallen Church out of her secular condition. Suddenly, his whole understanding of the theological task changed. Whatever the occasion for it, whether he himself suddenly realized that he was not communicating with his students, or whether he became convinced that the modern Protestant denomination would never shake its worldly character, Gilkey found himself looking at his own theological enterprise from the standpoint that he had previously criticized--namely, from that of a churchman who is aware that the world has indeed engulfed the Church! Gilkey must have understood rather abruptly why the denominations could not really appreciate his book. The talk about the "transcendent Word of God" did not make any impact on them because the word "God" was having no effect on them. It did not point to anything that made any difference whatever in their daily lives. It was meaningless!

With that realization the primary task of theology became for Langdon Gilkey how to make that single syllable "God" meaningful again. It was really to start from theological scratch. He could no longer assume that theology as an enterprise was of unquestionable worth, nor that the traditional language of theology conveyed universally shared meanings. In an article for <u>The Christian Century</u> in 1964, he described his experience of the change in theological posture as follows:

> The most significant recent theological development has been the steady dissolution of all these certainties, the washing away of the firm ground on which our generation believed we were safely standing. What we thought was solid earth has turned out to be shifting ice--and in recent years, as the weather has grown steadily warmer, some of us have in horror found ourselves staring down into rushing depths of dark water. [11]

As Gilkey came then to see it, the basic issue of theology in the twentieth century is to be joined at the very primary level of that which is the presupposition for all dogmas and all doctrines whatsoever--at the level of the question of

the reality of God Himself. One cannot read the literary result of his new theological posture, his book, Naming the
Whirlwind: The Renewal of God-Language, and escape the
impression that Gilkey was driven to this new posture, and
that it has caused him no little suffering and pain. His was
not a gleeful leap into the latest fashion in theology, but rather a sober recognition that a serious effort would have to
be made to gain access to the modern, secular minds of
churchmen for Christian faith. It carried him to the conviction that such an access could only come about by means of
a basic discussion of the meaning of God Himself, and that
such a discussion would have to employ a language that ap-
pealed to the ordinary experiences of human life.

It might be said that Langdon Gilkey experienced a
kind of theological future shock back in 1964. He found himself and his professional understanding overtaken by the new
age of radical secularism; yet, as with his experience in
Shantung compound, he was convinced that beneath the surface
of stark differences there was a basic continuity between his
old world and the new secularism. Both needed God. Secularism has not eliminated the search for the ultimate, the
need for grace, for unconditional acceptance which lies at the
heart of every human community. The new theological posture gestated for some five years and finally appeared as
Naming the Whirlwind, a long, repetitive work, but one rich
in human and theological insight. In it Gilkey remains a pro-
ber of the human heart after the order of St. Augustine.

NOTES

1. Langdon Gilkey, Shantung Compound (New York: Harper
   & Row, 1966), p. 4. Used by permission of the publisher.

2. Ibid., p. 230.

3. Ibid., p. 234.

4. Langdon Gilkey, How the Church Can Minister to the
   World Without Losing Itself (New York: Harper &
   Row, 1964), p. 2f. By permission.

5. Ibid., p. 17f.

6. Ernst Troeltsch, The Social Teachings of the Christian

Churches (New York: Macmillan, 1949), Vol. I, pp. 328-382 cited by Gilkey, Ibid. , p. 4.

7. Ibid. , pp. 1-20 for the analysis summarized here.

8. Ibid. , p. 19.

9. Ibid. , p. 20.

10. The Bible, Amos 8:11.

11. Langdon Gilkey, "Dissolution and Reconstruction in Theology, " The Christian Century, Feb. 3, 1965, and cited by Gilkey in Naming the Whirlwind, p. 8f, footnote 5. Used by permission of The Christian Century.

THE CRISIS OF "GOD" LANGUAGE*

by Langdon Gilkey

The Present Ferment

The suddenness and the radicalness of the present ferment in theology cannot be overemphasized. For four decades,
since 1918 or thereabouts, there had been going on what
seemed to the younger generation of theologians an immensely
creative and yet firmly based process of theological construction, fashioned by a remarkable group of brilliant minds:
Barth, Brunner, Tillich, Bultmann, and the Niebuhrs, to
name only a few. Those who stood closer to Barth drew
primarily upon Biblical and traditional sources for their constructive work; others reflected more a worldly or cultural
wisdom. But all together shared certain common assumptions
about the theological task which were communicated to their
enthusiastic younger followers: (1) that theology as an enterprise has both substance and integrity since, as a way of
reflecting on God, man, and destiny, it stems from a unique
and certain source in divine revelation, a source related to
in faith and so in direct experience, whereby the validity of
this viewpoint was assured: (2) that the reflective language
of theology is universally meaningful since, far from being in
conflict with legitimate cultural truths, it provides on the
contrary the basis for a more intelligible interpretation of the
totality of cultural experience than can any secular standpoint.

Theological construction thus springs ultimately from
faith, where its validity is known, and its implied meanings
include those foundational attitudes that form the presupposi-
tions of the furthest reaches of secular human inquiry and
knowledge: the natural sciences, the social sciences, philosophy of history, moral studies, psychology, literature, and

*From Naming the Whirlwind: The Renewal of God-Language,
copyright © 1969 by Langdon Gilkey. Reprinted by permission of the publisher, The Bobbs-Merrill Company, Inc.

the arts. Thus did the younger generation of theologians, whatever "school" they followed (Barthian, Niebuhrian, Tillichian, or even Whiteheadian), feel inwardly certain about the possibilities, the validity, and the universal meaningfulness of the theological language they were learning to use--and correspondingly, younger ministers or chaplains, and the theologically involved laymen whom they interested, had confidence that what they preached and expounded in church or college discussion groups had firm validity in, and immense relevance to modern life.

What has happened in the course of the last five years is that this whole relation to the great theological systems of the recent past has suddenly shifted. Unexpected new problems have arisen, and with their appearance younger theologians have found their own points of view uncomfortably changing, and so almost in an instant all these certainties about the established validity and meaningfulness of theological language have disintegrated.

An illuminating illustration of this radicalization of the debate over theological language is the fact that current questions concern more the meaning than the validity of theological discourse. To question the meaning of a fideistic or a metaphysical theological system is more radical than to question its validity. To say "I understand what you mean by belief in God, but I do not think it is true," is, to be sure, to deny the actuality of the Christian view; but it is at least to grant its possibility as one intelligible mode of understanding the world. We seem here to be agreeing that, while the world as we experience it might be as Christians describe it, nevertheless, because of such and such, we do not think in fact it is that way.

When, however, we question the meaning of the statements of faith or of metaphysics--when we say, "I do not even know what you mean by the word 'God'," or "I find metaphysical propositions meaningless"--we are not merely questioning the actuality or validity of these conceptual systems as explanatory of the experienced world. Rather, we are doubting even that they are intelligible at all as potential modes of understanding the world, we are doubting their possibility as explanatory or assertive conceptual systems. That is to say, we are in fact wondering whether, granted the modern view of things, such forms of belief or thought can even be conceived to fit at any point at all into the world as we actually experience it, and so a fortiori whether they can parade as modes of understanding that world.

The category "Meaningless" has been hard to define and in some quarters even abandoned in modern linguistic philosophy, especially after the demise of the verification principle; but, we believe, this lack of precise definition does not entail either the meaninglessness or the uselessness of the concept. What "meaninglessness" implies, we submit, is a sense of the total disrelation of a given set of concepts or a language game to experience and to life; and it is this total disrelation that is being asserted in the accusation that metaphysics or theology is meaningless--since it is clearly not their self-contradiction for which we are indicting them. Thus it is quite legitimate that, in relation to the question of meaning, there have arisen the various requirements or norms of verification and falsification, of "making a discernible difference, " of "counting for or against, " of usage in our ordinary discourse, and of relating our symbols to lived experience. All of these are ways, some better and some worse, of seeking to guarantee a relation of our concepts to experience and so to establishing at least a basic part of the meaning of the concepts involved.

When, therefore, we assert that viewpoints or conceptual systems are "meaningless, " what we are really saying is (1) that these assertions relate at no point to concrete experience, and (2) that therefore they are not possible modes of understanding experience. The first order of business, then, for contemporary theological reflection is, we feel, to deal with the problem of the meaning of religious language and through that avenue to approach the deeper issue of the reality of God.

Renewed "God" Language as the Language
of the Quest for Ultimacy

Our human story fluctuates back and forth between an idolatry and pride by which we raise our causes, our groups, and ourselves to the level of ultimacy and by which we achieve a sense of reality and community, and a disintegration and self-destruction in which we find in ourselves only nonbeing, stain, isolation, and hopelessness. Truly man is caught between heaven and earth, between an idolatrous being and the ultimate abyss of nonbeing, and his life swings back and forth between these two destructive ultimates. Our most fundamental searches, then, as transient fallible creatures, are

for an ultimate commitment in terms of which our contingen-
cy may be anchored against disintegration and unreality, and
for an ultimate acceptance and reconciling power through
which this inevitable process of self-rejection and inner dis-
unity can be stopped and reversed into creative community
with others.

   The writer realized anew the universality of this search
for innocence and reconciliation when one day he sat in a New
York City bus in front of two ladies, one of whom was regal-
ing the other with a story of a quarrel she had just had with
some third person who had been, apparently, a close friend.
It was clear that the quarrel had hurt the lady; its devasta-
ting effects on her sense of personal self-confidence, integrity, and of important communion with others were evident in
the emotional tone that covered every sentence and which obviously inspired the long recital. One hardly needed to hear
what was being said, for the way it was said revealed all the
important aspects of the recital. When she repeated to her
listener what her antagonist had said to her ("And so she said
to me ... "), the tone was hard, unyielding, hostile, and ag-
gressive--hearing those remarks said in that way, no one could
blame the teller for her angry reaction (in fact, I said to myself at that point, "Even St. Francis would have taken affront
at that!"). Then when she repeated what she had said in reply ("And so I said to her ... "), the tones vastly altered;
now they were quiet, infinitely tolerant, reasonable, and re-
conciling--no one could take offense at those reconciling remarks, or possibly misconstrue that outgoing warmth. The
tones themselves unmistakably proclaimed that the blame for
the angry explosion and the break in community, with which
the quarrel had ended, lay entirely with the other lady, and
that the raconteuse had been, in this situation--although mani-
festly innocent and the embodiment of love itself--deliberately
misunderstood, unfairly and gratuitously insulted, and then
brutally rejected by a ruthless, hostile foe. Obviously the
emotional point of the story was to establish, both to the new
friend who was listening and, above all, to herself, the blame-
lessness of this lady in the situation in which she felt momen-
tarily disunited in herself, fairly guilty, and suddenly socially isolated and alone. This long recitation (all the way from
122nd Street to 79th) was a vast effort to make the self ac-
ceptable again to itself, and to establish alliances amid seriously broken community. Both efforts were futile, as her
listener's neutral, wary, and uncommitted comments made
clear, and as her own obviously continuing sense of guilt evi-
denced. How could she convince herself of her innocence

when she herself had created this interpretation of past history, because she already knew herself to be partly to blame!

The futility of such efforts to generate the power to • accept ourselves and to recreate community is apparent: the others never accept our doctored accounts, and we who have censored and edited them are deeply aware that they are by no means the whole truth. Nor does it finally help if this acceptance by which we can accept ourselves comes from Mommy and Daddy, from their later surrogates, or even from our fellows: our friends, or our national, racial, or religious communities, however full of grace their love, forgiveness, and acceptance may be. In the first place, these immediate communities of acceptance are all too apt to share in and so to enlarge the conflicts that beset our communal life: in being accepted by our community we may be impelled into a wider and deeper conflict. But more profoundly, in receiving our own deepest acceptance from these others, we again lose our integrity and freedom, for the basis of our spiritual existence is thus surrendered to others and our final independence is forever gone. Again, integrity is achieved and preserved not only by community, but also by distance and separation as well. Finally, even the analyst can do this important task for us only temporarily, in the context of the session--and not for our continuing life as a whole. We seek for an ultimate acceptance by which we can live, yet one which neither we nor the humans around us can generate.

As our common experience continually validates, both the innocence that is demanded by our search for acceptance, and the forgiving love which resolves the issue--in Christian terms, both the law and the gospel--have an unconditioned character, else the healing for which we search cannot begin. For us to accept and love ourselves unqualifiedly and so creatively--whatever we are-- we must be loved and accepted unqualifiedly, and yet by an acceptance that we know to be valid, neither based on ignorance nor sentiment, one that knows both our guilt and yet still loves us. Again the finite--the self itself, the human friend, parent, or analyst, even the wider community itself--cannot answer this question or resolve this search without deluding us, on the one hand, or destroying our freedom, on the other. For what we need is not an acceptance based on the assurance of our innocence, as might now tell ourselves; what we need is forgiveness, i.e., a recognition of the guilt we know full well to be there, and then an awareness of a reconciling power that can both reintegrate our alienated self and our broken relations with others. Put in terms of Christian discourse, we are in all of this secular activity, common to the life of all of us, searching for God as forgiving and justifying love and as healing and sanctifying grace--though we may not be at all aware of this, and may see no possible relation of these older symbols heard in church to the problems in office, club, and family kitchen, as well as in our social and international conflicts, that worry and unnerve all of us.

And Christian witness would add that we will not be whole again until we find the unconditioned love, forgiveness, and re-creative power of God--though we cannot pretend to have established that through such an analysis of our ordinary life as this. It is probably by now clear, however, that only on the basis of having experienced our own fallibility and fault, and subsequently having discovered a healing acceptance of ourselves, that we can have a prophetic role against others in the world and for the oppressed therein, a role that is not hostile but creative. When we, too, have been forgiven for our sins, we may more hopefully embark upon becoming like Jesus to our neighbor in the world. Thus the cross is not only a sign of the negation of the world, but also necessarily a symbol of the negation of the virtue of the prophet himself.

Continuing for the moment further concerning the character and shape of Christian commitment and belief, we can say that it is especially in relation to these ultimate questions discussed in this context, "Who am I?" and "How can I be whole again?" that Christian existence has structured both its piety and its self-understanding. As a form of religious faith, it is based on the experience of answers to these two universal and quite secular human questions. In the Christian experience of an answer to these ultimate questions, the healing love and power of God are mediated to us through the figure of Jesus. We know it is God who is at work in this experience because no man in the distant past could so communicate to us in the alienated present the healing self-acceptance and the power to affirm and realize our own freedom. If he is to do this in and to us, and, as even the radical theology of our times witnesses, Jesus does this in Christian experience, then some power that underlies him and did not die with him, and now works anew through the present community in us, some power that transcends his passing and continues as the ground of our fleeting present, must come to us through this Lordly figure of the past. And only the forgiveness and grace of the source and ground of our life can heal us without destroying our autonomy and freedom; if we are dependent at all for our personal being on something beyond ourselves, on a Lord of any sort, it must be on God the creator of our free self that we depend, lest we lose our humanity all over again. Neither the categories of nature nor of historical community contain such an experienced power, nor express the ultimacy that is inherent in both the devastation of its absence and the blessing of its presence. Only the symbol of God, pointing as it does to the transcendent, the everlasting, and the unconditioned character of this love and this grace, can properly thematize in reflection that of which we are here aware in our existence.

We can, perhaps, say that a central part of what it is to be a Christian is to experience in these ways a unifying answer to all these common questions we have here begun to delineate. It is to know that the mysterious power from which our existence comes, and the mysterious destiny on which the meanings of our active lives are dependent, are to be understood as the same power and meaning that accepts, loves, and heals us through Jesus of Nazareth. In the love communicated to us through him, we know at last more clearly who or what it is that has created us and that rules our destiny. The mystery on which we depend, the "Holy Nothingness" that is the beginning, the middle, and the end, takes its shape, becomes "God" in the figure of Jesus Christ. Thus does he become "our Lord, " and the center of both our freedom and our existence, and thus do we begin to know of whom we speak when we say the word "God. "

The experience of the sacred and so our knowledge of what Christians name God are not separated from our secular life and its values. The sacred is dimly but universally experienced by all men everywhere as a source of that life's power and joy, the source of its meaning and structure, and finally wherever that experience is known, as the sole ground of that life's healing. And thus, in our Christian language about God, we can begin to talk of him in secular terms-- though by no means without difficulty--as the creator and ruler of our existence and above all as the father who in love comes to us in Jesus who is the Christ.

HANS KÜNG

THE CRISIS OF AUTHORITY

A Theologian of the Church

Hans Küng is the most controversial theologian in the Roman Catholic Church at the present time. In all likelihood he will remain so for some years to come. For this reason it may seem most inappropriate, even unfair, to present his views in a series of ecumenical studies. What complicates matters even more is the fact that the editor of these studies is a Protestant and Hans Küng has been dismissed by some of his critics within the Roman Catholic Church as a "Protestant," and what is apparently worse, "as a liberal Protestant."[1] But to leave the perspective of Hans Küng out of these studies would mean turning our eyes away from the storm center, from the heart of the crisis of faith in the Roman Catholic communion at the present time. It would amount to downright untruthfulness in so far as it is our intention to examine this crisis as understood by contemporary Roman Catholic theology. Furthermore, the controversial public career of Hans Küng cannot be treated as an isolated Catholic phenomenon apart from The Second Vatican Council. That career really began when he became one of the council's official theologians, each designated as "expert" (peritus).[2] Küng was thirty-four years old at that time, and considered but one of many promising young theologians of his Church. His role in the preparations for the Council soon catapulted him into the public eye.

Having received a licentiate in philosophy from The Pontifical Gregorian University in Rome in 1951, Küng then concentrated on theological studies. He was ordained a priest of the Roman Catholic Church in 1954 and received his licentiate in theology in 1955. His postgraduate program of study leading to his doctorate in theology was accomplished at the Institut Catholique in Paris. The dissertation for which he received his degree in 1957 was about the great Protestant theologian, Karl Barth. Entitled Justification: The Doctrine of Karl Barth with a Catholic Reflection, this work was acknowledged by Barth as a most competent exposition of his thinking. Küng had argued in the work that Barth's doctrine was in principle agreement with the traditional teaching of the Roman Catholic Church. Barth's admiration of this book established Küng in the eyes of many Roman Catholic theologians as a leading Catholic interpreter of Protestant theology.

Küng's continuing studies of Protestant theologians, especially of the reformers, Luther and Calvin, have in the course of the last decade made him suspect to many of his Catholic colleagues, but Küng has always argued for the catholicity of his own theology. If that catholicity should happen to agree with what Protestant theologians have also said, then truthfulness demands that this agreement should not be covered up, but rather used for the sake of Christian unity. However, in all fairness it must also be noted that Küng has not concealed his disagreement with Protestant theologians, especially where the latter may have tended to play down the significance of the resurrection of Jesus Christ for the Church. Küng has been anything but liberal Protestant in the centrality which he has accorded to the resurrection of Christ for Christian faith, as the following passage from his book, The Church, readily shows:

> The oldest circle of Jesus' disciples based its account, with considerable emphasis, on meetings which they really and unquestionably had with Jesus, whom God had raised from the dead. The Church sprang not from imaginings, not out of a baseless credulity, but from real experiences of encounters with one who was truly alive; but no interpretation of the disciples' witness can explain them away. Certainty replaces anticipation, affirmation replaces doubt. Jesus the preacher becomes Jesus the preached, the bearer of the message becomes the central substance of the message. Jesus is now recognized and acknowledged to be what he has now revealed himself to be: the Messiah (the anointed king, the Cristos, a word which was later attached like a second name to that of Jesus), the Son of Man descended from heaven, the Son of David, the Servant and Son of God, the Kyrios, the Lord (the name especially used in the hellenistic world).

> With this affirmation of faith a new community is
> born. [3]

The book that probably called the attention of the wider public to Küng was The Council, Reform and Reunion,
which he wrote and published well in advance of the first session of the Council. [4] The subtitle of the German edition,
which first appeared in 1960, was "Renewal as a Call to Unity." Here Küng called for a renewal of both Protestantism
and Catholicism according to the truth of the Gospel. Such
renewal would pave the way for a possible reunification in
the distant future which would neither ask Protestants simply to return to Mother Church, nor would expect the Roman
Catholic Church to capitulate to Protestantism. In addition
to extensive liturgical reforms, including the restoration of
the cup to the laity at mass on certain occasions, Küng
called for a re-examination of such matters as papal infallibility, celibacy, and the laws for marriage. He dared to
say that the power of the curia should be limited and that
broader powers be acknowledged as belonging to bishops.
He advocated the reform, or better yet, the abolition of the
Index of Prohibited Books, which Paul VI was actually to do.
In a section entitled "The Chief Difficulty for Reunification,"
Küng called for a renewal of the office of the Pope by dis-
sociating it from any suggestion of worldly aristocracy:
from imperial pomp, from the diplomacy of power politics
in worldly affairs, from the image of the chief bureaucrat. [5]
Küng suggested that such renewal had already begun when
Pope John, "against all tradition and completely unexpectedly," gave a homily on "The Good Shepherd" at his own in-
augural mass. [6] Pope John presented himself as "the Servant
of Servants" in true apostolic spirit. He asked the Church
to pray that he be humbled, and that he continue in true
evangelical humility. Here was a Pope exercising his genuine spiritual primacy in a way that encouraged Küng to issue his call for the renewal of the whole structural organization of the Church, including the Papacy.

By May of 1962, five months before the Council, Küng
had produced yet another book, Structures of the Church, in
which he entered into a detailed discussion of the issues he
had raised in his previous work. Küng was fast becoming
an expert on "ecclesiology" (the doctrine of the Church) and
on the history of the Church's institutional and dogmatic development with regard to its own self-understanding. This
was clearly demonstrated in a larger work, The Church,
published both in German and in English the same year,

1967. Since then a stream of publications has appeared under his name--all dealing with some facet of the task of Church renewal. The latest, and probably the most controversial book is Infallible? An Inquiry, published in the United States in the spring of 1971 by Doubleday and Company. In this work Küng repeated again his often stated contention that the Roman Catholic Church and her Popes have erred in the past, and added to it a short syllabus of errors as evidence. Whether Küng has indeed passed beyond the pale of Catholicism will depend upon how authorities in the Church interpret the following passage* from the book in which he argues that the special grace bestowed to the Church by God be understood as "indefectibility" rather than as "infallibility":

> We would like therefore to give preference to the concept of 'indefectibility' or 'perpetuity' in truth over that of 'infallibility.' The concept of 'indefectibility' (unshatterability, constancy) and the positive concept of 'perpetuity' (indestructibility, continuance) are just as much traditional concepts in ecclesiology as 'infallibility.' In practice they can often be scarcely distinguished. And if perpetuity or indefectibility in textbook theology have been linked more closely with the existence than with the truth of the Church, it must be remembered that the Church's being and being true simply cannot be separated from each other. If the Church is no longer in the truth, she is no longer the Church at all. But the Church's being true is not absolutely dependent on quite definite infallible propositions, but on her remaining in the truth throughout all--even erroneous--propositions. However, in order to bring out the fact that the Church's being means being true, for clarity's sake we shall speak, not simply of the indefectibility or perpetuity of the Church, but of her indefectibility or perpetuity in the truth. What is meant here then is that the Church remains in the truth, and this is not annulled by the sum total of individual errors. It should thus be clear that we are

*(From Infallible? An Inquiry by Hans Küng. Translated by Edward Quinn. English translation copyright © 1971 by Doubleday & Company, Inc. Reprinted by permission of the publisher.)

holding fast to the reality of infallibility, even
though for the reasons given we prefer the words
'indefectibility' or 'perpetuity' for the same reality.

In this way the word 'infallibility' would remain ultimately reserved to the one to whom it was originally reserved: to God, to His word and His
truth, to God who can neither deceive nor be de-
ceived and who alone is infallible in the strict
sense. [7]

This passage is an expression of the crisis of authority as Hans Küng sees it. The authority of the Church and
the stance of "being in the truth" are one and the same.
To the extent that the truth question is disregarded, or neglected, or in any way subordinated--to that extent there is
a loss of spiritual authority from the point of view of Christian faith, and a loss of credibility from the point of view
of unbelief. Küng is convinced that there is a radical difference between really "being in the truth" and a human
grasp of what it means to be in the truth. The Church ex-
presses its own grasp of what it means to be in the truth in
language: in propositions or statements of faith. To do this
it uses words and concepts that are provided by the culture
in which it finds itself. Other institutions of the culture
may use the same words and concepts, but for different purposes. An example would be the concept of authority as
used by a university, and again the same concept as used by
the state. Thus all words and concepts carry with them connotations which can conceivably lead to the misunderstanding
and misinterpretation of any proposition or statement made
by any official of the Church, including the Pope. Küng's
concern is to show that the intention of any proposition of
the Church cannot be infallibly communicated because of the
ambiguity of language itself. Thus for Küng the Church's
grasp of the truth is subject to distortion and error because
of the human capacities employed in any grasp of the truth
which comes to expression in language. But "being in the
truth" is for Küng a matter that transcends our ability to
grasp the truth. It means that God in His power and authority, in His faithfulness to the covenant with His people,
keeps and sustains His people in the truth of the covenant,
even when they err, sin, or present a distorted understanding of that covenant. In statements and propositions, men
express their grasp of the truth; by His own faithful activity
in the providential care of His people, God grasps His people. This is what Hans Küng means by indefectibility. "[8]

For Küng it is fitting for a Church aware of its being grasped by the Truth of God, of its being in the truth, to question its own grasp of that truth. It bespeaks genuine humility. A Church that refuses to question its own grasp of the truth, on the other hand, ends up exalting itself, breaks itself away from the serious quest for truth, and thus loses credibility. Hans Küng is thus saying for the Church in our day what St. Augustine said to the Christians of his day who were worried about alien, cultural influences on the Church: "Let every good and pious Christian understand that wherever he finds truth, it is his Lord's."[9] The way to unity, then, is the way of being in the truth, which means being always engaged in the serious quest for truth wherever one may be. It means that one is really free to ask of himself, have I genuinely grasped the truth of how God is caring for His Church in truth?

A test of whether the Church genuinely understands its own being in the truth is whether it is really free to confess its past mistakes, its own sins committed often in the name of possessing the truth. Küng's bedrock conviction is that what the Church says about the truth of faith, or the "deposit of faith," will be taken with the same degree of seriousness by the world at large and by other religious communities that the Church itself displays in telling the truth about its own past development and its own way of being in the world right now. If the story that the Church tells covers up and conceals the mistakes and errors in a self-serving way, those who know the historical truth can only be repelled. They become the offended "little ones" about whom Jesus spoke when he said, "... But whoever causes one of these little ones who believe in me to sin, it would be better for him to have a great millstone fastened around his neck and to be drowned in the depth of the sea." (Mt. 18:6.)

Unless the Church tells the truth about itself, Catholic churchmen who know better may find themselves in the horrible self-contradiction of having to use the truth of the Church against the Church and thus place themselves in danger of dismissing the earthen vessel, the finite means chosen by God to bring them to truth in the first place. Küng has seen how many have been so offended and left the Church, but he himself refuses to do so. In this steadfast remaining with the Church that he so often criticizes, Küng shows himself to be a true son of Roman Catholicism. In an article for the magazine, America, entitled "Why I Am Staying in the

Church, " Küng emphasized the fact that there is so much in the church and its tradition that he can affirm. He acknowledged how much he is at home in the community, in spite of all that might be raised against its hierarchical apparatus. The abuse and misuse of the structures of the Church are reasons for remaining and struggling in the truth of the Church. [10]

Küng is a theologian determined to spend the truth, the riches of the Church, always for the Church, and never against it as a reason for leaving. He is also very aware that the fallibility which he finds in the Church's statements also applies to his own theology. He knows that he not only could be, but has been wrong many times in his attempt to grasp the meaning of being grasped by the Truth of God; therefore, he welcomes discussion and correction by other members of his community of faith.

The following selections show Küng's basis for Christian truth-telling about the Church's sins--namely the activity of The Holy Spirit, which, according to Küng, may never be simply identified with the Church, even as the Church as a community may not understand itself apart from the activity of the Spirit. The question then is, what is the activity of the Spirit? Küng answers it in very concrete terms. The selection under the heading "The Church and the Jews" is an example of the sort of truth-telling that Küng is constrained to do as part of his witness to the freedom of the Church under the reign of the Holy Spirit. These selections are an indication of how Küng proposes to restore the credibility of the Church in an age that is all too conscious of the all too human dimension of the Church.

NOTES

1. So Karl Rahner was quoted by Newsweek Magazine, Jan. 24, 1971, p. 57.

2. This designation was reported as part of Küng's biography in Current Biography, 1963, p. 228.

3. Hans Küng, The Church (New York: Sheed and Ward, 1967), p. 80. Used by permission of Sheed and Ward for the U. S. and possessions, and by Search Press Ltd. for the British Commonwealth.

4. Hans Küng, The Council, Reform and Reunion (New York: Sheed and Ward, 1962). This was first published in German under the title: Konzil und Wiedervereinigung: Erneuerung als Ruf in die Einheit (Freiburg und Basel: Herder Wien, 1960).

5. Ibid., (German Edition), pp. 161-182, especially p. 177f.

6. Ibid., p. 177f.

7. Hans Küng, Infallible? An Inquiry (Garden City, New York: Doubleday and Co., 1971), p. 182f.

8. For an American discussion of the issues raised by Küng, see John J. Kirvan, ed., The Infallibility Debate (New York and Paramus, N. J.: The Paulist Press, 1971).

9. St. Augustine, On Christian Doctrine, tr. D. W. Robertson, (New York: The Bobbs-Merrill Co., Inc., 1958), Book Two, Ch. XVIII, par. 28.

10. Hans Küng, "Why I am Staying in the Church," America, March 20, 1971, p. 282.

THE HOLY SPIRIT: THE BASIS FOR THE CHURCH'S CONFESSION OF SIN*

by Hans Küng

The Church under the Reign of the Spirit

The distinction between Spirit and Church has its basis in the divine nature of God's spirit or, as we can also put it, in its freedom. Spirit and Church, however closely linked, are not on the same plane; the Church is subordinate to the Spirit of God. This distinction of freedom can be summed up in four sentences:

1. The Spirit is not the Church. It would be dangerous to try and identify the Church and the Holy Spirit; for the Holy Spirit is the Spirit of God, not of the Church; hence the fundamental freedom of the Holy Spirit. Just as the Holy Spirit, although it dwells in a Christian, is not identical with the Christian's spirit, so the Spirit is not the Spirit of the Church but of God. There is no mention in the New Testament of the Holy Spirit as the "Spirit of the church, " only as the "Spirit of God, " as the "Spirit of Jesus Christ. " This Spirit proceeds not from the Church nor from an individual Christian, but from God. It is not the possession or property of the Church, nor its power and strength, but God's. Through him God acts in the Church, reveals himself and comes to the Church, provides a foundation for the Church and sustains it. He governs the Church, but never becomes the Church's own spirit, nor merges with it. He remains God's own Spirit and for this reason is and remains

*From The Church by Hans Küng, © Verlag Herder KG, Freiburg im Breisgau, 1967; English translation © Burns & Oates Ltd. , 1967; published by Sheed & Ward Inc. , New York. Translated by Ray and Rosaleen Ockenden. Reprinted by permission of Sheed & Ward for the United States and possessions, and by Search Press Ltd. for the British Commonwealth.

the free Spirit.

We are the Church, we the fellowship of men who believe in Christ. We, the Church, are a human structure.
But the Holy Spirit is divine, not human. For all the links
between them there is no identity, but rather a fundamental
distinction between the Spirit of God and the human structure
of the Church. This difference is not merely a general and
abstract one, the ontic difference between the divine and the
human. The real Church, of which we are speaking, is not
only a Church composed of people, but of sinful people. The
real Church is not only human, but also sinful. We are the
Church, justified but sinful men, we, the fellowship of the
righteous who are yet constantly dependent on forgiveness:
communio sanctorum indeed, but also regrettably always the
communio peccatorum. * So the Church is sinful. The Spirit of God on the other hand is not sinful, but the Holy, the
completely Holy, Spirit. Hence the Spirit is in this very
much deeper sense also the free Spirit, truly free from sin,
guilt and death.

* * *

To avoid confusing the Spirit and the Church, it would
be better not to speak of the Church as a "divine" reality.
The individual believer, after all, does not become a "divine"
reality because he is filled with and governed by the Spirit.
It would also be better not to speak of an organic development of the Church and its spirit. The romantic and idealistic view of Church history overlooks the fundamental difference between the perfect Spirit of God and an imperfect
Church. It is because of the distinction between the Spirit
and the Church that its development often includes developments in the wrong direction, and progress often includes
retrogression. Finally, to avoid confusing the Spirit and the
Church, it would be better not to speak of the "sense of the
faithful" (sensus fidelium) in the Church as though it were a
revelation of the Holy Spirit. The Church's sense of the
faith can never be a source and a norm of the revelations of
the Spirit. On the contrary: revelations of the Holy Spirit
provide the source and norm of the Church's sense of faith.
These concrete examples show that the Holy Spirit in the
Church is and remains a free Spirit.

---

*Editor's note: Communio sanctorum is communion of saints;
communio peccatorum is communion of sinners.

It is obvious how important this distinction is. The Church does not per se and in each case represent the Holy Spirit; the Church has to prove its holiness in action. Only by accepting the distinction can we truly face up to the all too human aspect of the church, its failures and shortcomings, its sin and guilt, in a proper liberating way. A Church which identifies itself with the Holy Spirit cannot say the Confiteor.* It cannot, may not, confess that it has sinned in thought, word and deed, through its fault, through its most grievous fault. It will be forced into unsound theological prevarications and apologetics which convince no one. In short, it will fall prey to an idealistic and triumphalist conception of the Church which is full of illusions. And it will therefore not be a free Church.

Only by drawing this distinction can we really listen to God's word in the Holy Spirit and be obedient to the Holy Spirit, in a truly liberating way. A Church which identifies itself with the Holy Spirit has no need to listen, to believe, to obey. It turns itself into a revelation, it knows and does everything. It needs only to listen to itself, to obey itself and believe in itself, and urge others outside the Church to listen, believe and obey. In short, it will fall prey to a self glorifying and egocentric conception of the Church, and again it will be anything but a free Church.

But a Church which distinguishes between itself and the Holy Spirit can face up to sin and failure in the Church soberly and humbly, but also with the liberating hope of those already justified that they will be forgiven anew. A Church which draws this distinction will believe, obey and hope without putting its trust in itself, but precisely in God's Holy Spirit. A Church which proudly identifies itself with the free Spirit of God is a Church which for all its vaunted strength is ultimately weak, for all its imagined freedom is ultimately unfree. But the Church which humbly distinguishes itself from the free Spirit of God is for all its undeniable weakness strong, and for all its apparent unfreedom ultimately free.

*   *   *

2. The Spirit precedes the Church. The Holy Spirit

---

*Editor's note: Confiteor is the Church's confession of sin in the mass.

is not an external extra to the Church, as though the Church could exist without the Holy Spirit, although perhaps only in an imperfect and unvital way. When Scripture refers to the Church as a spiritual house, as a temple of the Holy Spirit, it does not mean that the Church is the outward form or framework into which the Spirit, the living content, then entered. The Church is not something which competent and clever ecclesiastical organizers, administrators and big business men can work out and set up, after which the Holy Spirit can find in it a centre of operations or even a resting-place.

The Spirit of God comes first; and through the Spirit God in his freedom creates the Church, and constantly creates it anew from those who believe: "No one can say 'Jesus is Lord' except by the Holy Spirit" (I Cor. 12:3). Through the operation of the Spirit the Church is created and created afresh each day: emitte spiritum tuum--et creabuntur!* There is no Christian existence which is not created and must constantly be created; and none is created without the operation of the Spirit. Of course, there is no Church without the decision of believers and their free gathering together. But the believers who congregate in the Church do not summon themselves. They do not even summon themselves to faith. God himself calls them through the word of Christ in the power of the Holy Spirit to faith and hence to the Church as the fellowship of the faithful. God in the Holy Spirit acts in perfect freedom. The beginning is his, as is the continuation and the end. Everything is his, who in the freedom of his power and strength remains the sovereign Lord of the Church.

3. The Spirit works where he wills. The Spirit of God cannot be restricted in his operation by the Church; he is at work not only in the offices of the Church, but where he wills: in the whole people of God. He is at work not only in the "holy city," but where he wills: in all the churches of the one Church. He is at work not only in the Catholic Church, but where he wills: in Christianity as a whole. And finally he is at work not only in Christianity, but where he wills: in the whole world.

The power of the Spirit of God can pass through all walls, even church walls. It is true that the Holy Spirit has

---

*Editor's note: "Send your Spirit, and they shall be created!"

his dwelling and his temple in the Church, which he fills
and which he governs. Here his power is especially revealed, since in the Church and through the Church the word
of God is preached and his sacraments are administered.
But the Spirit of God, if domiciled in the Church, is not do-
mesticated in it. He is and remains the free Spirit of the
free Lord not only the "holy city, " not only of Church offices, not only of the Catholic Church, not only of Christians,
but of the whole world.

* * *

4. The Spirit is at work when he wills. The Spirit
of God is not, of course, a Spirit of arbitrariness or apparent freedom, but of real freedom; he is a Spirit of order,
not chaos; peace, not contradictions, in the Church as well
as in the world. This is what Paul had to remind the Corinthians, who, proud of their spiritual gifts, had neglected order in the Church: "God is not a God of confusion but of
peace" (I Cor. 14:33). Arbitrariness, disorder and chaos
in the Church cannot be the work of the Holy Spirit.

At the same time, God's Spirit does not blow when
he must, but only when he wills. No decrees of the Church,
in doctrine or practice, can force him to act or not to act
at a given time. True, God is absolutely free, and is thus
free even with regard to his freedom. He is so overwhelm-
ingly free, that he can bind himself, as he does indeed in
word and sacrament. But by being bound to word and sacrament he affirms not his limitations or unfreedom, but his
all-powerful, abundant freedom.

God's Spirit knows no law but that of his own freedom, no authority but that of his own grace, no power but
that of his own faithfulness. God's Spirit is at all events
not bound by the laws or authority or power of the Church.
God's Spirit is not ruled by ecclesiastical laws or authority
or power. He himself reigns and rules sovereign over
them. Anyone in the Church who supposes he can dictate
to the spirit on the basis of law, authority or power must
necessarily fail. The Church cannot take over the Spirit,
or in any real sense "possess" him, control or limit, direct or dominate him.

The Church cannot do any of these things, either
through its word or its sacraments. God binds himself in
the Spirit to word and sacrament, not on the basis of the

Church's authority but on the basis of his free grace; not on
the basis of the Church's power, but on the basis of his
faithfulness. The fact that God binds himself to word and
sacrament of the Church, lays an obligation not on him but
on us. We do not demand something of him, he demands
something of us: our unconditional faith. Neither word nor
sacrament works automatically where there is no faith; they
are not operative. Anyone who thinks that the Spirit can be
compelled with word or sacrament, or with law and authority, power or order, is leaving out of account precisely that
faith which the Spirit demands of him: faith not in his or
the Church's law, authority, power or order, but in God's
free grace and faithfulness. It is true therefore of the
Church too that the Spirit blows not when he must, but when
he wills.

* * *

The Church cannot dictate to the Spirit or regiment
it. It can only pray and beg: Veni! God's Spirit may
dwell in the spiritual house of the Church, and remain with
the Church and work through it. But he dwells and remains and works there not on the basis of a law, because
he must, but on the basis of his faithfulness, because he
wills. "He who calls you is faithful, and he will do it"
(I Thess. 5:24).

We, who are the Church, must never forget that we
are sinners, albeit justified, and must constantly be aware
of the fact; we live therefore in contradiction to God's spirit, we "grieve" him and can, from our viewpoint at least,
lose him. We must not forget that our faith though it may
give us certainty, is constantly threatened and challenged;
we can only trust in God's faithfulness and grace. It is by
no means automatic that the Spirit should remain with us,
the Church. All we can do is to pray penitently, not only
"veni sancte Spiritus" but also "mane sancte Spiritus, " remain with us, despite our faithlessness, because of your
faithfulness. The Church, despite its constant failures, has
never lost the free Spirit of God in all its members; this is
not something to be taken for granted, it is the miracle of
God's faithfulness, which we can never take for granted but
must constantly believe and pray for anew.

The Church and the Jews

Gentile hostility to the Jews, especially as a result

of the religio-political nonconformism of the Jews, existed before Christianity. The same complaints were made about Christians up to the third century, but nevertheless the enmity between Jews and Christians increased. Various interacting factors played an important part in this: (1) the increasing distance of the Church from its Old Testament roots as a result of the hellenization of the Christian message; (2) the exclusive commandeering of the Old Testament by a Church which no longer valued the Old Testament in its own right, but by means of typological and allegorical interpretation turned it almost entirely into a prophecy of the Christian religion; (3) guilt for Jesus' crucifixion and death, which was generally attributed to the Jews and all Jews, and taken as the reason why the whole race had been cursed, rejected and condemned to dispersion; (4) the breakdown of any dialogue between Church and synagogue, growing isolation, and the substitution for dialogue of an apologetic monologue.

The formation of the imperial Church under Constantine brought a further development. On the basis of the uniqueness of their God as revealed in the Old Testament, and especially on the basis of their expectation of a Messiah and the kingdom of God, the Jews had always rejected the hellenistic and Roman imperial cult and the whole myth of the empire--an essential reason for Gentile hostility to the Jews. In the same way they now rejected the christianized ideology of the empire, according to which the emperor and his rule was an image and continuation of the heavenly reign of God. Specifically Gentile hostility to the Jews was now taken over by the imperial Church, which had conveniently forgotten its own days of persecution, and strengthened considerably by the introduction of Christian ideas. The laws of the imperial Church effectively banished Jews from the sacral kindgom, to which entry could only be obtained through the sacraments: mixed marriages were forbidden, as was the holding of official posts by Jews, the building or extension of synagogues, etc. So the Jews within the empire were in practice living outside the empire. While some theologians like Augustine still saw the Church as having a missionary duty towards the Jews, others like Chrysostom were already making inflammatory attacks upon the Jews in the style of the later anti-Jewish preachers. The Corpus iuris civile of Justinian, which intensified the anti-Jewish measures of Theodosius in particular, became a cornerstone of all medieval laws about Jews.

The historic prejudices against the Jews which were
repeated right down to most recent times are in part very
old, in part of medieval origin; their lack of foundation is
well known: "Jews are only interested in money" (cf. the
colloquial sense of the word "Jew"). But it was the Christians who drove the Jews out of their official posts, out of
the judiciary and the army, and in addition denied to them
farming and crafts. Jewish landowners were not allowed to
use Christian workers, Christian guilds closed all crafts to
the Jews. In this way they compelled them to take up trading in money, as the only way they could eke out their existence. Almost everything--the right to come and go, to
buy and sell, to communal prayer, to marry and to bear
children--the Jew had to pay for in cash. Only in recent
times, with the setting up of the state of Israel, has the old
idea that Jews were incapable of farming and craft-work
been clearly refuted.

"The Jews are damned to perpetual homelessness"
(cf. the legend of the wandering Jew Ahasuerus, condemned
because of Jesus to wander and never die); But the Jewish
diaspora had begun several centuries before the death of
Jesus. At the time of Jesus' birth only a fraction of Jews
were living in Palestine. On the other hand, a large number of Jews continued to live in Palestine both after the destruction of Jerusalem by the Romans and after the revolt
of Bar-Kochba. It was not until the crusaders came that
they were reduced to a tiny remnant who lived a penurious
existence as dyers. Here again the foundation of the state
of Israel has demonstrated the untruth of this legend.

"The Jews are criminals" (cf. the fables of ritual
murders, of the poisoning of wells; of sacrilege against the
sacred host; or the dangerousness of Jewish doctors (cf.
the "plot" of Jewish doctors on the life of Stalin in 1953).
But all these general accusations are without foundation; in
the Old Testament and Talmud alike we find a horror of defilement through blood; medieval emperors like Frederick II
and popes like Innocent IV defended the Jews against attacks
of this kind centuries ago.

These often laughable, but at root highly dangerous
prejudices and legends cost countless Jews their lives. In
1348-9, the time of the worst persecutions of the Jews in
the Middle Ages, about 300 Jewish communities in Alsace
and in the Rhineland, in Thuringia, Bavaria and Austria
were destroyed, and the rest lived there on sufferance.

Why? The rumour had started in southern France that Jews had poisoned the wells and were therefore responsible for the plague which had broken out. In 1290 the Jews were expelled from England, in 1394 from France, in 1492 from Spain, in 1497 from Portugal.

But the terrible persecutions, expulsions and mass murders of the later Middle Ages by no means ended with the Reformation. Luther, particularly, in his later writings, wrote more violently against the Jews than many of his predecessors. In his notorious pamphlet "The Jews and their Lies" (1543) he called for the burning of their synagogues, the destruction of their houses, the confiscation of their sacred writings; he proposed that they should be forbidden on pain of death to teach or hold services, that safe-conduct should be denied them, that their possessions should be seized. Even though Calvin's whole theology emphasized the unity of the covenant, and even though in the Reformed Churches as a whole there was a respect for Judaism, under the influence of humanism, this did not materially affect the preaching and catechetics of these Churches.

But despite these changes [brought about by a few more tolerant people in the eighteenth century], hostility to the Jews had by no means been overcome in the Church and in society at large. In the East there were numerous violent persecutions of the Jews and as a result of the Russian and Polish pogroms, many Jews fled to the West and to America. For German idealism, notably for Hegel, Judaism figured as the manifestation of the evil principle. It needed merely the race-theories of men like Gobineau and Houston Stuart Chamberlain to provide the ideological basis for a racist "anti-Semitism." As a result of various economic, political and ideological factors this led to the unparalleled and fearful explosion of "anti-Semitism" in National Socialism. The Nazi atrocities reduced the number of Jews in the world by a third. About six million Jews, men, women and children, were gassed and annihilated. At the turn of the century 80 per cent of all Jews lived in Europe; in 1958, 34 per cent.

Of course, not all the guilt for the sufferings of the Jews can be laid at the door of the Church. They were often caused by heathens both then and now, who were against Israel's God. And in spite of all the heathen elements which crept into the Church, there has always been, particularly in recent times, vocal Christian protest and courageous opposition to all "anti-Semitic" hatred and all inhumanity. But too often this protest was made by individuals or outsiders, while official representatives of the Church, and often its highest dignitaries, withdrew into cautious, politic and opportunistic silence, or spoke only hesitantly and softly, in words which were diplomatically shrouded in qualifications, and failed to display any prophetic power or spirit of commitment; words, in short, which fell short of the Gospel of Jesus Christ. But it is important to see beyond the individual case and to realize that Nazi anti-Semitism, however much it may have been primarily the work of godless and criminal men, would have been impossible without the preceding two thousand years of "Christian" hostility to the Jews, which hampered Christians in offering convinced and energetic resistance to it on a broad front.

Only one thing is of any use now: a radical metanoia, repentance and re-thinking; we must start on a new road, no longer leading away from the Jews, but towards them, towards a living dialogue, the aim of which is not the capitulation but simply the understanding of the other side; towards mutual help, which is not part of a "mission, " to an encounter in a true brotherly spirit.

Part II

THEOLOGIES OF EVOLUTIONARY CHANGE

TEILHARD DE CHARDIN

A ROMAN CATHOLIC EVOLUTIONARY THEOLOGY

The Phenomenon: Teilhard de Chardin

A glittering intelligence, a spirit soaring in its quest for truth, a genuine reverence for life--all this and more converged in the person of Teilhard de Chardin. He was at once a poet, philosopher, scientist, and theologian-priest, a man uniquely equipped for a life of study and reflection in the twentieth century. More than that of any other single individual, Teilhard's thought influenced the content of the Vatican II document, "The Pastoral Constitution on the Church in the Modern World." The statement, "... the human race has passed from a rather static concept of reality to a more dynamic evolutionary one,"[1] probably would not have been written, had it not been for the widespread knowledge of his works in Roman Catholic intellectual circles and in the world at large. By 1965, when Pope Paul VI promulgated this pastoral constitution, the posthumously published writings of Teilhard were so generally acclaimed by theologians and secular thinkers alike that his thinking had become a phenomenon for the Church to reckon with. To have evaded the issues raised by his writings would have meant evading reality. The Church's response at Vatican II proved that it had chosen the course of facing up to the new understanding of life and reality.

Pierre Teilhard de Chardin was born at the Chateau de Sarcenat in the province of Auvergne, France in 1881. He died in New York City in 1955, at the age of 74. From childhood his life was shaped by his concern for both science and religion. In the Jesuit school that he entered at the age of ten his special interests were geology and mineralogy, which he pursued along with the usual humanistic and religious studies. When he was eighteen he entered the Society of Jesus, which was expelled from France during the early years of his training.   Upon completing his preparatory studies in Jersey, he went to Cairo in 1905 and there spent the next three years teaching chemistry and physics.   After that he went to England where he completed his studies for the priesthood.

World War I found him at the front lines serving as a stretcher-bearer in the thick of the fighting.   This experience impressed him with the basic unity of all mankind underlying the tragedies perpetuated by war.   After the war he returned to his scientific studies and in 1920 he became Professor of Geology at the Catholic Institute of Paris.   In 1923, during his first scientific expedition to China, his group made the exciting discovery of the remains of an ancient man commonly referred to as "Peking man."   Back in Paris in 1924 he found that his teaching was suspect to his superiors because of his understanding of original sin and its relation to evolution.   He was forbidden to teach and later to publish his writings.   Under these conditions he was permitted to return in 1926 to China where he resumed his studies of the earliest stages of the earth's existence and of organic life.   He remained there for some twenty years, writing the works that would be published only after his death in 1955.   He would have returned to Paris in 1938 to assume the duties of director of a laboratory for advanced studies in geology and palaeontology, but the outbreak of war between China and Japan prevented his return until 1946.

His superiors in his order were no more hospitable to his ideas after World War II than they had been in 1924. Forbidden once again to publish or to teach, he continued his independent researches, and traveled to other countries. In 1951 he moved to New York where he helped to formulate anthropological policy for the Wenner-Gren Foundation. Though he was often appreciated more by his secular colleagues than by his co-religionists, Teilhard remained an obedient priest throughout his career.   He never broke the official silence imposed upon him, nor did he question the authority of his Church to command it.   Yet, he was sure that his contribution was as much to theology as it was to science.   Before his death he made arrangements for the posthumous publication of his writings.   The Phenomenon of Man, his most important work, was published in French the year of his death, and it appeared in English in 1959 with an introduction by none other than Sir Julian Huxley, the noted scientific opponent of Christian orthodoxy. [2]   By 1966 nine volumes of his scientific essays, religious reflections, and letters were available in French and English, with more still to be published. The book most clearly reflecting his personal spirituality is The Divine Milieu.[3] Today there is a Teilhard de Chardin Society in each of several nations, including France, Ireland, and the United States. They are all ecumenical in composition and character, and they are carrying on with his task of synthesizing scientific and theological reflection.

Teilhard's Vision of Evolution

In 1905 a Methodist theologian by the name of Olin Curtis published his systematic theology, entitled The Christian Faith. In it he addressed himself to many of the same questions that were to animate Teilhard's thinking. At one point, Curtis wrote:

> As an individual, a man is a part and a very important part of the natural universe. The cosmos becomes complete only in him. Indeed, there is, I sometimes think, a secret cosmic force, not yet caught by science, which binds together every created thing, and makes us all from men to rocks into one vast mystic organism.[4]

This statement sums up very well Teilhard's basic conviction, which he articulated in The Phenomenon of Man. What Curtis called "a secret cosmic force, not yet caught by science," Teilhard called simply energy, but his conception of energy is so radically different from the prevailing scientific concepts of energy that one would still have to say that science as an enterprise has still not caught, clarified, and applied Teilhard's concept of energy. For Teilhard, too, it is the basic force that binds everything from rocks to men, from the simplest crystals to the most complex of organisms, into one throbbing, pulsating universe of life. In hope of aiding and not discouraging the reader, a brief statement of his basic evolutionary principles is included here along with his fundamental picture; however, it is also hoped that the passages selected from Teilhard's own writings will have some meaning for the reader who has no background in science.

First, let us consider Teilhard's conception of matter and of motion. In his picture, all existing things consist of matter, which in all things betrays certain common characteristics. These common characteristics of matter are elaborated differently in different things, thus demonstrating different stages or levels of complexity. These characteristics are both formal and behavioral--that is, matter can be grasped in terms of basic form and at the same time in terms of how it moves or behaves. When matter appears, both of these characteristics are presented together for observation. Teilhard stated it as follows:

> To begin with, at the very bottom there is still an unresolved simplicity, luminous in nature and not to be defined in terms of figures. Then, suddenly came a swarming of elementary corpuscles, both positive and negative (protons, neutrons, electrons, photons): the list increases incessantly. Then the harmonic series of simple bodies, strung out from hydrogen to uranium on the notes of the atomic scale. Next follows the immense variety of compound bodies in which the molecular weights go on increasing up to a certain critical value above which, as we shall see, we pass on to life. There is not one term in this long series but must be regarded from sound experimental proofs, as being composed of nuclei and electrons. This fundamental discovery that all bodies owe their origin to arrangements of a single initial corpuscular type is the beacon that lights the history of the universe to our eyes. In its own way, matter has obeyed from the beginning that great law of biology ... the law of 'complexification.'[5]

These general characteristics of all things, subject to scientific observation, Teilhard called "the without of things."[6]

Teilhard's new, and often perplexing, discussion of "energy" appeared under the heading "The Within of Things."[7] According to him, all energy is physical in character, but energy behaves in two distinct ways. In its physical character energy is "the measure of that which passes from one atom to another in the course of their transformations."[8] The two ways in which he understood matter as behaving were defined according to the direction of the movement of energy. One direction is outward on a level of the same atomic structure. The result is that elements "of the same complexity and the same centricity" are linked together.[9] Teilhard called energy moving in this direction "tangential energy," and identified it as the energy that science generally describes in terms of the laws of thermodynamics.[10]

The other direction in Teilhard's conception of energy is the one that is a matter of scientific dispute. Here, as Teilhard saw it, energy moves in the direction of ever greater complexity and ever greater centricity, or, as he put it, "forwards."[11] Energy moving in this direction is the force which thrust out of inanimate matter to produce animate nature. It accounts for the changing complexities in the tendency towards centeredness, given with matter itself, which in the course of evolution has appeared as consciousness in animals, and as self-consciousness, as person, at the level of man. This "within of things" is thus the secret cosmic force which unites everything in a living universe. Teilhard called it "radial energy."[12]

Teilhard's conception of "radial energy" provided him with two of the basic principles of his theory of evolution. One was the principle of "embryogenesis," according to which each stage of evolution is understood as having been present implicitly in all preceding stages. Teilhard stated it as follows: "Everything, in some extremely attenuated extension of itself, has existed from the very first."[13] Elsewhere he wrote:

> In the world, nothing could ever burst forth as final across the different thresholds successively traversed by evolution (however critical they be) which has not already existed in an obscure and primordial way. If the organic had not existed on earth from the first moment at which it was possible, it would never have begun later.[14]

The other principle derived from his conception of radial energy is "orthogenesis." According to this principle, evolution is moving upward, in an ascent towards the greatest centricity and greatest complexity. It accounts for the movement from micro-molecule to the mega-molecule to the living cell. To Teilhard, it suggested that evolution is moving in a "predetermined direction,"[15] which meant for him an ultimate, final center, which he called "point Omega." He was convinced that life by its very nature is progressive. He expressed this conviction as follows: "Without orthogenesis life would only have spread; with it there is an ascent of life that is invincible."[16]

Teilhard's picture of evolution is the concretization of matter in motion. At any given stage or level of complexity energy spills out in a swarming effect, producing a vast multiplicity of like structures. During this swarming, radial energy is also present, albeit more subdued. As the swarming effect subsides, radial energy increases, building in the direction of greater centeredness and complexity. The result: evolution moves up to a whole new level of centeredness and complexity, and the swarming effect begins again. Energy moving in this broad pattern was Teilhard's way of accounting for a "long series of complex substances" that can be found between two extremes: one in the center of stars in whose extreme temperatures matter exists in its most simple dissociated state; the other in the barysphere, the depth of the earth where the metals also display "this relative simplicity of chemical bodies. "[17]

Teilhard saw the complex structures between these extremes as "harboured and produced only by stars that have 'gone out.'"[18] Geogenesis, the formation of the earth, occurred as the slow and gradual complexification of the matter of a dead star. In the course of this development, tangential swarming and radial complexification produced successive zones. Over the barysphere a siliceous zone appeared, forming the hard crust of the planet. Then came a zone of water and carbonic acid, totally enclosing the core and crust of the earth "in an unstable, mobile and penetrating envelope."[19] The result was definable layers: barysphere, the lithosphere (crust), hydrosphere (oceans), atmosphere, stratosphere, and beyond that the ionosphere with its layers of electrically charged molecules.

The existence of these zones together in their various stages of complexity was for Teilhard the necessary condition for biogenesis, or the emergence of organic life. In Teilhard's picture, "life no sooner started than it swarmed."[20] It formed a film of micro-organisms that spread over the earth. Tangential and radial energy burst forth on a new plane, producing the flora and fauna of the earth. It is important to remember that for Teilhard this new envelope, which he called the biosphere, emerged from within the complexity of the interaction of the other zones, and maintains itself in that "within." The apex of the biosphere, which becomes the occasion for the next great turn of evolution to a whole new stage, is the appearance of man. The spread of mankind throughout the earth in a way that superimposed a specifically human reality over it was called the process of "planetization" by Teilhard. The process whereby man became a unique organism through the development of the capacity for self-grasp and self-reflection, he called "hominization." Entailed in this latter process is the complex social organization of mankind which is made possible because of man's peculiar consciousness.

The new stage of evolution occasioned by the appearance of man is the emergence of consciousness, or mind. Teilhard saw it as a whole new sphere which could only be understood as a new kind of "envelope" enclosing everything else, yet emerging from out of the complexity within the interaction of everything else. His word for this sphere is the "noosphere," or the sphere of mind, which is a new occasion for energy to move toward a new kind of complexity and centeredness--collective thought. It is of the nature of mind, or spirit, to be aware of the process of evolution itself. Self-conscious evolution thus begins to grope, to seek a center beyond all of the centers. This new center he saw as Omega, the point of ultimate convergence, the final completion of the process of cosmogenesis, or the becoming of the world and everything entailed in it.

The occasion for the movement of mind toward point Omega in Teilhard's picture of the world is the appearance of the Christ. Through him consciousness is raised through faith, hope, and love towards God as the point Omega. The sphere of mind, the noosphere, is thus transformed into the "divine milieu."

Here, in Teilhard's vision of evolution, science and theology, knowledge and faith are seen as ultimately converging. From the viewpoint of the secular scientist, the priest in Teilhard was victorious. From the viewpoint of many Churchmen unwilling to come to terms with the evolutionary character of reality, the scientist in him was victorious, recasting all of Christian doctrine in terms of evolution. Which of these interpretations is correct, or whether in the last analysis truth was victorious in his writings, the reader must decide for himself.

NOTES

1. Cited in the Introduction above, p. 8.

2. Teilhard de Chardin, The Phenomenon of Man (New York: Harper & Row, 1959).

3. Teilhard de Chardin, The Divine Milieu (New York:

Harper & Row, 1960).

4. Olin A. Curtis, The Christian Faith (1st edition, New York: Eaton and Mains, 1905; published again, Grand Rapids: The Kregel Publications, 1956 and 1971), p. 105. Reprinted by permission of The Kregel Publications.

5. The Phenomenon of Man, p. 47f. Reprinted by permission.

6. Ibid., p. 55.

7. Ibid., Ch. 2, pp. 53-74.

8. Ibid., p. 42.

9. Ibid., p. 64f.

10. Ibid.

11. Ibid., p. 65.

12. Ibid.

13. Ibid., p. 78.

14. Ibid., p. 71. Used by permission.

15. Ibid., p. 108.

16. Ibid., p. 109. See Garret Hardin, Nature and Man's Fate (New York: Mentor Book, 1959), p. 226, for a discussion of orthogenesis from a biologist's point of view. He claims that the often used chart of evolution of the horse from a small to a large animal is misleading. The fossil record now indicates that the horse grew larger and smaller many times in the course of evolution.

17. Ibid., p. 68.

18. Ibid.

19. Ibid.

20. Ibid., p. 92.

THE WORLD, MAN AND GOD*

by Teilhard de Chardin

The World

First and foremost, the world is still building.

That is the basic truth which must be grasped at the outset and assimilated so thoroughly that it becomes part of the very habit and nature of our thought. At first sight we might be tempted to think that created beings and their destinies are dispersed at random, or at any rate arbitrarily, over the face of the earth. We could almost believe that each one of us might equally well have been born earlier or

---

*The selection under the heading "The World" is from "The Meaning and Constructive Value of Suffering, 1933, " translated by Noel Lindsay and published in Pilgrim of the Future: a Teilhard de Chardin Symposium, edited by Neville Braybrooke (New York: Seabury Press, 1964; London: Darton, Longman & Todd, 1966). Reprinted by permission of Neville Braybrooke.

The selections under the headings "Man" and "God, the Omega" are from The Phenomenon of Man by Pierre Teilhard de Chardin, translated by Bernard Wall. Copyright 1955 by Editions du Seuil. Copyright © 1959 in English translation by Wm. Collins Sons & Co., Ltd., London, and Harper & Row, Publishers, New York. All citations in this volume from this work reprinted by permission of the publishers.

The selection under "The End of the World" is from The Future of Man by Pierre Teilhard de Chardin, translated by Norman Denny. Copyright 1959 by Editions du Seuil. Copyright © 1964 in the English translation by William Collins Sons & Co., Ltd., London, and Harper & Row, Publishers, New York. Selection from pp. 306-308 reprinted here by permission of the publishers.

later, here or there, richer or poorer, as though the universe from the start to finish of its history were some vast pleasure garden in time and space, in which the gardener could change the flowers about at his own sweet will. But ideas of this kind will not hold water. The more we reflect, in the light of the lessons to be learned from science, philosophy, and religion, each in its own sphere, the more we realize that the world is to be likened, not to a gathering of individual elements, assembled with art, but rather to some organic system, animated by a broad movement of growth, special to itself. Over the centuries an all-embracing plan seems in truth to be unfolding around us. Something is afoot in the universe, some issue is at stake, which cannot be better described than as a process of gestation and birth: the birth of the spiritual reality formed by the souls of men and by the matter which they bear along with them. Laboriously, through the medium and by virtue of human activity, the new earth is gathering its forces, emerging and purifying itself. No, we are not like the blooms in a bunch of flowers, but rather the leaves and blossoms of some great tree on which all things appear in due season and due place, in time with and at the behest of the All.

Man

From our experimental point of view, reflection is, as the word indicates, the power acquired by a consciousness to turn in upon itself, to take possession of itself as of an object endowed with its own particular consistency and value: no longer merely to know, but to know oneself; no longer merely to know, but to know that one knows. By this individualization of himself in the depths of himself, the living element, which heretofore had been spread out and divided over a diffuse circle of perceptions and activities, was constituted for the first time as a center in the form of a point at which all the impressions and experiences knit themselves together and fuse into a unity that is conscious of its own organization.

Now the consequences of such a transformation are immense, visible as clearly in nature as any of the facts recorded by physics or astronomy. The being who is the object of his own reflection, in consequence of that very doubling back upon himself, becomes in a flash able to raise himself into a new sphere. In reality, another world is born. Abstraction, logic, reasoned choice and inventions, mathematics, art, calculation of space and time, anxieties and dreams of love--all these activities of inner life are nothing else than the effervescence of the newly-formed center as it explodes onto itself.

This said, I have a question to ask. If, as follows from the foregoing, it is the fact of being "reflective" which constitutes the strictly "intelligent" being, can we seriously doubt that intelligence is the evolutionary lot proper to man and to man only?

* * *

With the advent of the power of reflection (an essentially elemental property, at any rate to begin with) everything is changed, and we now perceive that under the more striking reality of the collective transformations a secret progress has been going on parallel to individualization. The more highly each phylum became charged with psychism, the more it tended to "granulate." The animal grew in value in relation to the species. Finally at the level of man the phenomenon is precipitated and takes definitive shape. With the "person," endowed by "personalization" with an indefinite power of elemental evolution, the branch ceases to bear, as an anonymous whole, the exclusive promises for the future. The cell has become "someone." After the grain of matter, the grain of life: and now at last we see constituted the grain of thought.

* * *

Thus, through this leap of intelligence, whose nature and mechanism we have been analyzing in the thinking particle, life continues in some way to spread as though nothing had happened. According to all appearances, propagation, multiplication and ramification went on in man, as in other animals, after the threshold of thought, as busily as before. Nothing, one might think, had altered in the current. But the water in it was no longer the same. Like a river enriched by contact with an alluvial plain, the vital flux, as it crossed the stages of reflection, was charged with new principles, and as a result manifested new activities. From now onwards it was not merely animated grains which the pressure of evolution pumped up the living stem, but grains of thought. What was to happen under this influence to the color or the shape of the leaves, the flowers, the fruit?

* * *

We have been following the successive stages of the same grand progression from the fluid contours of the early earth. Beneath the pulsations of geo-chemistry, of geo-tec-tonics and of geo-biology, we have detected one and the same fundamental process, always recognizable--the one which was given material form in the first cells and was continued in the construction of nervous systems. We saw geogenesis promoted to biogenesis, which turned out in the end to be nothing else than psychogenesis.

With and within the crisis of reflection, the next turn in the series manifests itself. Psychogenesis has led to man. Now it effaces itself, relieved or absorbed by another and a higher function--the engendering and subsequent devel-opment of all the stages of the mind, in one word noogenesis. When for the first time in a living creature instinct perceived itself in its own mirror, the whole world took a pace forward.

As regards the choices and responsibilities of our ac-tivity, the consequences of this discovery are enormous. As regards our understanding of the earth they are decisive.

Geologists have for long agreed in admitting the zonal composition of our planet. We have already spoken of the barysphere, the central and metallic, surrounded by the rocky lithosphere that in turn is surrounded by the fluid lay-ers of the hydrosphere and the atmosphere. Since Suess, science has rightly become accustomed to add another to these four concentric layers, the living membrane composed of the fauna and the flora of the globe, the biosphere, so of-ten mentioned in these pages, an envelope as definitely uni-versal as the other "spheres" and even more definitely indi-vidualized than them. For, instead of representing a more or less vague grouping, it forms a single piece, the very tissue of the genetic relations which delineate the tree of life.

The recognition and isolation of a new era in evolu-tion, the era of noogenesis, obliges us to distinguish correl-atively a support proportionate to the operation--that is to say yet another membrane in the majestic assembly of tellu-ric layers. A glow ripples outward from the first spark of conscious reflection. The point of ignition grows larger. The fire spreads in ever widening circles till finally the whole planet is covered with incandescence. Only one inter-pretation, only one name can be found worthy of this grand phenomenon. Much more coherent and just as extensive as any preceding layer, it is really a new layer, the "thinking layer," which since its germination and the end of the Tertiary period, has spread over and above the world of plants and animals. In other words, outside and above the biosphere there is the noosphere.

With that, it bursts upon us how utterly warped is every classification of the living world (or, indirectly, every construction of the physical one) in which man only figures logically as a <u>genus</u> or a new family. This is an error of perspective which deforms and uncrowns the whole phenomenon of the universe. To give man his true place in nature it is not enough to find one more pigeon-hole in the edifice of our systematization or even an additional order or branch. With hominization, in spite of the insignificance of the anatomical leap, we have the beginning of a new age. The earth "gets a new skin." Better still, it finds its soul.

* * *

The consciousness of each of us is evolution looking at itself and reflecting.

* * *

Man is not the center of the universe as once we thought in our simplicity, but something much more wonderful--the arrow pointing the way to the final unification of the world in terms of life. Man alone constitutes the last-born, the freshest, the most complicated, the most subtle of all the successive layers of life.

* * *

"There is nothing new under the sun," say the despairing. But what about you, O thinking man? Unless you repudiate reflection, you must admit that you have climbed a step higher than the animals. "Very well, but at least nothing has changed and nothing is changing any longer since the beginning of history." In that case, O man of the twentieth century, how does it happen that you are waking up to horizons and are susceptible to fears that your forefathers never knew?

In truth, half our present uneasiness would be turned into happiness if we could once make up our minds to accept the facts and place the essence and the measure of our modern cosmogonies within a noogenesis. Along the lines of this axis no doubt is possible. The universe has always been in motion and at this moment continues to be in motion. But will it still be in motion tomorrow?

Here only, at this turning point where the future substitutes itself for the present and the observations of science should give way to the anticipations of a faith, do our perplexities legitimately and indeed inevitably begin. Tomorrow? But who can guarantee us a tomorrow anyway? And without the assurance that this tomorrow exists, can we really go on living, we to whom has been given--perhaps for the first time in the whole story of the universe--the terrible gift of foresight?

Sickness of the dead end--the anguish of feeling shut in ...

This time we have at last put our finger on the tender spot.

What makes the world in which we live specifically modern is our discovery in it and around it of evolution. And I can now add that what disconcerts the modern world at its very roots is not being sure, and not seeing how it ever could be sure, that there is an outcome--a suitable outcome--to that evolution.

*   *   *

Either nature is closed to our demands for futurity, in which case thought, the fruit of millions of years of effort, is stifled, still-born in a self-abortive and absurd universe. Or else an opening exists--that of the super-soul above our souls; but in that case the way out, if we are to agree to embark on it, must open out freely onto limitless psychic spaces in a universe to which we can unhesitatingly entrust ourselves.

Between these two alternatives of absolute optimism or absolute pessimism, there is no middle way because by its very nature progress is all or nothing. We are confronted accordingly with two directions and only two: one upwards and the other downwards, and there is no possibility of finding a halfway house.

On neither side is there any tangible evidence to pro-

duce. Only, in support of hope, there are rational invita-
tions to an act of faith.

At this cross-roads where we cannot stop and wait
because we are pushed forward by life--and obliged to adopt
an attitude if we want to go on doing anything whatsoever--
what are we going freely to decide?

God, The Omega

We have seen and admitted that evolution is an ascent
towards consciousness. That is no longer contested even by
the most materialistic, or at all events by the most agnostic
of humanitarians. Therefore it should culminate forwards in
some sort of supreme consciousness. But must not that
consciousness, if it is to be supreme, contain in the highest
degree what is the perfection of our consciousness--the illuminating involution of the being upon itself? At first sight
we are disconcerted by the association of an Ego with what
is the All. The utter disproportion of the two terms seems
flagrant, almost laughable.

* * *

Are we not at every instant living the experience of
a universe whose immensity, by the play of our senses and
our reason, is gathered up more and more simply in each
one of us? And in the establishment now proceeding through
science and the philosophies of a collective human world-
view in which every one of us co-operates and participates,
are we not experiencing the first symptoms of an aggregation
of a still higher order, the birth of some single center from
the convergent beams of millions of elementary centers dispersed over the surface of the thinking earth?

All our difficulties and repulsions as regards the opposition between the All and the Person would be dissipated
if only we understood that, by structure, the noosphere (and
more generally the world) represent a whole that is not only
closed but also centered. Because it contains and engenders
consciousness, space-time is necessarily of a convergent
nature. Accordingly its enormous layers, followed in the
right direction, must somewhere ahead become involuted to
a point which we might call Omega, which fuses and con-
sumes them integrally in itself.

* * *

... it would be mistaken to represent Omega to ourselves simply as a centre born of the fusion of elements
which it collects, or annihilating them in itself. By its
structure Omega, in its ultimate principle, can only be a
distinct Center radiating at the core of a system of centers;
a grouping in which personalization of the All and personal-
izations of the elements reach their maximum, simultane-
ously and without merging, under the influence of a supremely autonomous focus of union. That is the only picture
which emerges when we try to apply the notion of collectiv-
ity with remorseless logic to a granular whole of thoughts.

The End of the World

... It is difficult to imagine what form the ending of
a World might take. A sidereal disaster would correspond
nearly enough to our individual deaths. But this would entail
the ending of the Earth rather than of the Cosmos, and it is
the Cosmos itself that must disappear.

The more I ponder this mystery the more it assumes
in my dreams the aspect of a "turning inward" of consciousness, an eruption of interior life, an ecstasy. There is no
need for us to rack our brains in trying to understand how
the immensity of the material universe might vanish. It is
enough that the spirit should be reversed, that it should enter another sphere, for the face of the world to be instantly
altered.

As the end of time approaches a terrifying spiritual
pressure will be brought to bear on the limits of the Real,
born of the effort of souls desperately straining in their desire to escape from the Earth. This pressure will be unan-
imous. But the Scriptures teach us that at the same time
it will be rent by a profound schism between those who wish
to break out of themselves that they may become still more
masters of the world, and those who, accepting Christ's
word, passionately await the death of the world that they may
be absorbed with it into God.

And no doubt it is then, in a Creation brought to the
paroxysm of its aptitude for union, that the Parousia [return
of Christ] will occur. The unique process of assimilation
and synthesis, pursued from the beginning of time, being at
length revealed, the universal Christ will appear like a flash
of lightning amid the storm-clouds of a slowly consecrated

World. The trumpets of the angels are but a weak symbol. It is in the grip of the most powerful organic attraction conceivable (the force which held the Universe together!) that the monads will pour into that place whither they are irrevocably destined by the total maturing of all things and the implacable irreversibility of the whole history of the World-- some of them spiritualised matter in the limitless fulfillment of an eternal communion, and others materialised spirit in the conscious agonies of an interminable decomposition.

At this moment, St. Paul tells us (I Corinthians IV, 23 et seq.), when Christ shall have emptied of themselves all the powers created (rejecting that which is an element of dissociation and super-animating all that is the force of unity) He will consumate the universal unification by delivering Himself, in His entire and adult body, with a capacity for union that is at length perfected, to the embrace of the Deity.

Then the organic complex will have been constituted of God and the World, the Pleroma--the mysterious reality that we cannot do better than call simply God, since although God might dispense with the world we cannot regard it as being wholly an accessory without rendering Creation incomprehensible, the Passion of Christ meaningless and our own struggle uninteresting.

Et tunc erit finis. [And then the end will come.]

Like a vast tide the Being will have dominated the trembling of all beings. The extraordinary adventure of the World will have ended in the bosom of a tranquil ocean, of which, however, each drop will still be conscious of being itself. The dream of every mystic will have found its full and proper fulfillment. Erit in omnibus omnia Deus. [God will be all in all.]

NORMAN PITTENGER & JOHN COBB

PROTESTANT PROCESS THEOLOGY

Faith Seeking Understanding in Our Time

When in 1924 the renowned British mathematician Alfred North Whitehead left Cambridge, England to teach at Harvard University in America, a new chapter began in the history of western ideas. At the age of sixty-three the wide-ranging thinker turned his attention from mathematics and science to perplexing questions of philosophy and religion, and he began to reflect on the cultural-historical context for both. Whitehead's move to Harvard proved to be an "occasion" such as he himself was to describe as the key concept of his process philosophy. From his new position at Harvard he looked back and gathered the significant knowledge of his years of study and research in science, philosophy and history, and then brought it to bear in his new situation in such a way that a new school of philosophy was created. At the center of this new occasion in western thought was Whitehead's awareness of a cultural conflict between the claims of science and religion. Enhancing the personal pain that he felt in the presence of this conflict was his own need to find a satisfactory way to reconcile science and religion because of the high value that he placed upon both. As he put it in his book, Science and the Modern World, published the year after his arrival in America:

> ... When we consider what religion is for mankind, and what science is, it is no exaggeration to say that the future course of history depends upon the decision of this generation as to the relation between them. We have here the two strongest forces (apart from the mere impulse of the various senses) which influence men, and they seem to be set one against the other--the force of our religious intuitions, and the force of our impulse to accurate observation and logical deduction. [1]

71

Here, in his apprehension about the future course of human civilization, he articulated the basic concern that was to produce what is now generally known as "Whiteheadian process philosophy."

In what must have been an amazing burst of creativity Whitehead laid the groundwork for the new school of thought in the first five years of his American career. (He died in 1947 in his eighty-sixth year). In 1926 his work Religion in the Making was published, in 1927 Symbolism, Its Meaning and Effect, and in 1929 Process and Reality, An Essay in Cosmology, all published by Macmillan and Co. Princeton University Press published The Function of Reason in 1929. Collections of his essays in science, philosophy, and related subjects were published in 1929, 1947, and 1961,[2] and two more books in 1933 and 1938.[3]

Whitehead's writings of the late 1920's attracted a great deal of attention and were generally acclaimed by other scholars who were already thinking along the same lines. But the theologians and philosophers who were willing to be identified with his philosophy and employ it in their own efforts were few in number. A small group of scholars who applied, with varying degrees of consistency, Whitehead's concepts in their interpretations of religion across the years earned for the University of Chicago a reputation as a center of Whiteheadian thinking. The group included Henry Nelson Wieman, Bernard E. Meland, Bernard M. Loomer and Charles Hartshorne. At most theological schools and in most philosophical faculties in America there were no representatives of Whitehead's process philosophy. Dr. Norman Pittenger, who taught for thirty-three years at General Theological Seminary (Episcopal) in New York City before going to Cambridge University in England, and Daniel Day Williams of Union Theological Seminary in New York City carried the torch for it in the east, where strong winds blew against it from continental Europe. The waves of Protestant neo-orthodox theology, especially of Emil Brunner and Karl Barth, created a climate hostile to Whitehead's thinking even in those Protestant theological schools with a reputation for high academic standards.

Those few who were dedicated to the articulation and further elaboration of process philosophy were not without their influence. Their students carried this view of reality into many other schools in the 1950's as they earned their degrees, usually at Chicago, and became teachers of philos-

ophy and theology.   Charles Hartshorne and his former students, Schubert M. Ogden, now at Perkins School of Theology in Dallas, and John B. Cobb, Jr. of the School of Theology at Claremont, California, have been particularly able
advocates of process thinking for theological reflection. [4]
Because of their mastery of Protestant continental theology,
Ogden and Cobb have become the chief interpreters of process theology to their colleagues in Germany.

In the last five years an increasing number of scholars and students have turned to process thought as the most
viable way to proceed in theology today.   An excellent an-
thology of process thinking, edited by Delwin Brown, Ralph
E. James and Gene Reeves, attests to this new vitality.
Called **Process Philosophy and Christian Thought**, it provides
the reader with samples of the earliest and the most recent
works of process thinkers and demonstrates as well the interest of Roman Catholic theologians in the enterprise.   The
essay by Gene Reeves and Delwin Brown, "The Development
of Process Theology," is a particularly illuminating account
of the history of process thinking in the American scene. [5]
It is recommended for those who are stimulated by, and
even enjoy, abstract conceptual thinking.   As a group, process thinkers can be characterized by their intellectual power, their broad-gauged interests cutting across many fields,
and the value that they place on reasoned discourse.   These
are precisely the qualities that do not endear them to many
of their opponents who in debate often find themselves backed
into a logical corner.

The very technical language of process philosophy poses a special problem for anyone approaching it for the first
time.   For this reason, Norman Pittenger's most readable
account of the basic assumptions of process thought and its
value for Christian theology was chosen for this context, as
was also John Cobb's discussion of the importance of God as
"the One Who Calls us into the future."   While these selections hardly do justice to the scope and complexity of process
thought, they may, as is to be hoped for all of the writings
in this volume, serve as a lure for further reading on the
subject.

NOTES

1.   Alfred N. Whitehead, Science and the Modern World
     (Copyright, 1925, by The Macmillan Company, New

York), p. 252f. Reprinted by permission of The
Macmillan Company for the United States and possessions, and by permission of Cambridge University Press for the British Commonwealth.

2. The collections of essays are: The Aims of Education
   and Other Essays. Macmillan, 1929; Essays in
   Science and Philosophy. Philosophical Library, 1947;
   The Interpretation of Science: Selected Essays, ed-
   ited with an Introduction by A. H. Johnson. Bobbs-
   Merrill, 1961.

3. The other books are: Adventures of Ideas. Macmillan,
   1933; Modes of Thought. Macmillan, 1938.

4. John Cobb's basic contribution, in addition to his many
   articles listed in a bibliography included at the end
   of Process Philosophy and Christian Thought by
   Brown, James and Reeves, is A Christian Natural
   Theology (Philadelphia: Westminster, 1965). A more
   popular version of his thinking can be found in God
   and the World (Philadelphia: Westminster, 1969),
   from which the selection offered here was taken.
   In his book The Structure of Christian Existence
   (Philadelphia: Westminster, 1967) Cobb interpreted
   the work of Christ in terms of process thought.
   Schubert Ogden's interpretation of process theology
   can be found in his essays published under the title
   The Reality of God (New York: Harper & Row,
   1966).

5. Delwin Brown, Ralph James, Gene Reeves, Process
   Philosophy and Christian Thought (New York:
   Bobbs-Merrill, 1971), pp. 21-64.

PROCESS-THOUGHT AND CHRISTIAN THEOLOGY*

by Norman Pittenger

The Assumptions of Process Thought

What are the assumptions with which process-thought begins? And why should Christian thinkers be interested in process-thought? Here are two preliminary questions to which we should turn before we begin our exposition of the attitude which process-thought in its wider significance takes towards problems such as the nature of deity, the meaning of divine activity in the world, and the nature of man and society.

The first and perhaps the basic assumption of the kind of interpretation of the world which we are here considering, is simply that we are confronted, both in our own human experience and in the description of things with which modern scientific enquiry has made us familiar, with a dynamic rather than with a static reality. Those who take this view would say, for example, that it is absurd to speak of "human nature" as if it were an entity that could be described in categories of substance, if by substance we mean immutable and unchanging thing. Man is "on the move"; he is a living, changing, developing creature. If he is to be described at all, the dynamic quality of his existence must be recognized and grasped, even if it is also the fact that through all the changes there are persistent qualities which preserve his identity as human. Likewise the world of nature is not a static affair in which things "continue in one stay"; on the contrary, it is evolving, changing, "in process." Down to the lowest levels of matter, if we may so

---

*Condensed with permission of The Macmillan Company from Process Thought and Christian Faith by Norman Pittenger. Copyright © 1968 by Norman Pittenger. Permission to reprint this abridged version outside of the United States and Canada was granted by James Nisbet & Co., Ltd. of London.

style them, this capacity for and presence of change and development is to be seen. Indeed Professor Whitehead was
prepared to go so far as to say that the electron itself is a
"society" or an "organism, " marked by movement and dynamic activity. Of course the sense in which such words
may be used to describe the various levels in the world will
vary according to the particular level which is under consideration at any given time and by any particular science. An
electron is not a dynamic society or organism of the same
order as an amoeba; certainly it differs vastly from the activity which we note in a living cell, in a plant, in a dog,
and a fortiori in a man. Yet the world as a whole is in
process and is a process; it is not a finished and settled
system composed of discrete entities which are inert,
changeless, static.

We are led then to a second assumption which is
basic to process-thought. Not only is the world and all that
is in it a dynamic movement; it is also an inter-related society of "occasions. " Nor is there the possibility of isola-
ting one occasion from another, so that each may be considered in itself alone. On the contrary, it would be a "false
abstraction" from the deliverance of experience and of observation to attempt to do this. Into each of the given occasions there enter past events as well as the surrounding
and accompanying pressures of other occasions, not to mention the "lure" of the future. To illustrate once again from
the area best known to us, this is obvious enough at the human level. A man does not and cannot exist in complete
isolation from other men, or from his present environment,
or from his own past history and the more general history
of the human race of which as man he is a part, or from
the natural order to which he and his whole race belong, or
from the possible developments which are before him and
mankind in general. Each man is a focusing, a concreti-
zing, of all these. Thus in being "himself" he is not himself alone; he is all that has gone to make him up, all that
surrounds him, all that presses upon him, all that he himself
enters into and in which he shares, all which he may be.
And that which is true of man is likewise true in its appropriate way throughout the universe. We live in and we are
confronted by a richly inter-connected, inter-related, inter-
penetrative series of events, just as we ourselves are such
a series of events. Whatever is our own specific identity,
it can be asserted of us only when this fact of our sociality,
of our organic nature, is grasped and given due emphasis.
The same must be said of the world as a whole.

This means that we are not able to make sharp dis-
tinctions of an ultimate and definitive kind. We cannot do
this between "selves, " for (as we have seen) they are inter-
penetrating. It also means that in the rich experience which
we possess, as we grasp it in that kind of double awareness
which Whitehead calls "presentational immediacy" and "causal efficacy, " we are given a full and compresent encounter
with the world. Hence it is impossible, for instance, to reject the aesthetic and valuational elements in experience, as
if these were to be seen as merely "subjective, " while the
primary qualities of hardness, etc., are taken as genuinely
"objective. " The fact is that our experience gives us all
this together, as being profoundly one in impact upon us;
we cannot cut up the world of experience, after the fashion
of an earlier philosophy, and speak as if that which in its
aesthetic quality has subjective appeal must lack any genuine reality in the world itself, simply because it does not
lend itself to a particular kind of analysis by measurement
or testing. It is of course true that we can and do make
abstractions. We are obliged to make them for practical
purposes as well as for a theoretical understanding of this
or that special question; but they are exactly what they are
called; they are "abstractions" from the richness of experi-
as we concretely know it.

This many-sided experience as it presents itself to us
in its immediacy carries with it the corollary of "causal efficacy. " By this process-thought (as expounded by Whitehead) means that there is given to us, in our experience at
all levels (including our "bodily" as well as our intellectual
awareness), the sense of a variety of relationships which
have played upon us and brought our experience to us in the
particular way in which in fact it has been brought. Causa-
tion, then, is to be taken as another word for describing the
way in which given occasions are brought to a focus and in
which they make their impact upon those to whom they are
presented. This rather than that to a focus is a genuine and
necessarily given factor which is present in whatever it is
that we are experiencing, sensing, feeling, knowing, understanding. What in an older kind of philosophy would have
been called the chain-of-cause-and-effect is here seen as being very much richer; it is a congeries of occasions, events,
pressures, movements, routes, which come to focus at this
or that point, and which for their explanation require some
principle that has brought and still is bringing each of them,
rather than some other possible occurrence, into this particular concrete moment of what we commonly style "existence. "

But what secures such persistence or identity in occasions as we do in fact know, both from observation and
from our own experience of ourselves? The answer to this
question is given in the concept of the "subjective aim"
which is proper to each series of occasions. This aim,
which has always about it a directive quality, is to be understood as the goal or end towards which a given process
moves, yet it must also be seen as in some sense imma-
nently at work in that process moving it towards its goal or
end or actualization. There is an element of teleological
concern in all process-thought, whether or not the particular description we have offered is accepted. But this does
not mean that each set of occasions is "conscious," in anything like our human sense, of the aim which is before it
and which gives it the distinctive identity that it possesses.
An acorn is certainly not aware of the "aim" which keeps it
moving towards its proper development into an oak-tree.
But none the less, what does thus keep it moving towards
its proper development is the subjective aim which is proper
to the acorn. And so, in appropriate measure and of course
with vast differences at each level, throughout the cosmos.
Thus we are delivered from a purely mechanical view of the
universe, in which nothing is going on but the re-shuffling of
a series of originally given entities. Yet we are not delivered into the hands of the vitalist who would wish to intro-
duce some kind of mysterious psyche or entelechy or spirit
(or whatever equivalent term he might use) as an addition to
the process. God himself is possessed of a subjective aim;
and every entity in the process, understood as dynamic,
inter-related, inter-penetrative of every other entity (and
hence better described as an occasion or instance along some
"route"), is also characterized by such an aim. This is a
truly organic and hence integrative view of "the way things
go."

Finally, because of the nature of the world as we
know it, we cannot grasp it with that kind of absolute clarity which a Cartesian type of thinking would demand. Indeed
we must always seek clarity, as Whitehead once said; but he
went on to say that at the same time we must always dis-
trust it. For the difficulty is that simple explanations,
which tend always to assume an omnicompetent knowledge,
are likely to give us falsely simple explanations. If we accept experience as we know it, there will be some things
which will appear relatively clear, but they will be set in
contexts which are not so clear. Hence the picture of truth
is much more that of a small area of fairly straightforward

knowledge which shades out into more and more mysterious and unclear knowledge or intimation or hint or apprehension, than it is that of "clear and distinct ideas" which leave no room for doubt and presume to give a simple and direct explanation of any given moment of experience.

The Value of Process-Thought for Christian Theology

Our second preliminary question concerned the reason or reasons why Christian thinkers should be interested in process-thought. An approach to an answer may be found by mention of a particular insistence found in one way or another in all thinkers of this school. Professor Whitehead has used the term "importance" to describe this insight, but there are many other possible ways in which it may be stated and other process-thinkers have their own terms to describe it. But using Whitehead's word, we may say that "importance" is appropriately employed to indicate the fact that some specific occurrence, some particular event or series of concrescent events, some particular stance or attitude, provides for any responsible thinker the "clue" which he takes for his understanding of "how things go." For example, we are all aware of the way in which a moment in the life of a man which to him seems to have decisive importance will give him his criterion of interpretation for all that happens to him. Some historical event, as we well know, can have a determinative significance for our comprehension of a whole series of preceding and succeeding historical events. That which in this sense is "important" not only seems to sum up or to crystallize (so to say) our prior experience, but also opens up for us new avenues of possibility, leading to future interpretations which will be enriching and deepening in our experience. Even more significant, the "important" will actually inaugurate a new level of understanding and thus give rise to a new level of experience for us and for those who follow us. It has an objective as well as a subjective quality. To this concept of "importance" we shall return in other contexts. At the moment it is helpful in our endeavor to see why process-thought has interest for Christian theology.

The point is of course obvious. The Christian believes that in the events of which Scripture is the record, and supremely in the events which find their focus in the life and activity of Jesus Christ, there is a disclosure of something which in the highest degree is "important." Since the Christian is convinced that this is the case, a kind of philosophy which is congruous with such a conviction should be very welcome indeed. Furthermore, if it can be shown that there are many points in which the Christian conviction of what is "important is illuminated by such a philosophy, the Christian will inevitably have more than academic interest in the way in which that philosophy interprets the world and human experience.

It would seem that there is a remarkable correspondence between the biblical insistence on the living God who is active in nature and in the affairs of men, and the recognition by process-thought that the world is a dynamic process of such a kind that whatever explanatory principle or agency there may be must be of that sort too--it also must be dynamic and processive. The Jewish-Christian tradition has never really been content with an "unmoved mover" as the final principle of explanation, however often the notion has been found in classical theologies. It has been uneasy when the God about whom it talks is described in substantial terms of a kind which leave little room for his boundless energizing activity in the world; it has been obliged to seek all sorts of verbal devices for putting life into such language. Process-thought in fact is much closer to the biblical way of seeing things, with its recognition of the profound importance of activity, movement, and development.

Furthermore, the whole creation itself, both what we call nature and also the realm of historical happening, is for the biblical writers open at every point to the action of the living God. They do not see it as a fixed entity, already made and finished; for them the creation is a directed movement in which novelty occurs, in which the unexpected may and indeed often does happen, and in which great ends are in process of achievement. A view of the world which regards it as a finished product has little relation to the world as the Bible sees it; while a world that is nothing but a complicated mechanism, like a machine which grinds along engaged in nothing but repeating standard patterns of behaviour, is not the world of movement and change of which the Scriptures speak. The Bible tells us of a faithful God whose purpose is unchanging; hence whatever he does will be consistent with his ultimate objective, while the created world will not be the scene of irrelevant and meaningless intrusions. But with all his faithfulness God is living and active, and the creation is not a "finished" world, much less a dead and inert substance. Granted once again that the biblical witness is in highly pictorial terms and that its "science" is outmoded, the fact yet remains that the biblical witness is to what we have styled an "open" world in which new things occur; that biblical witness always recognized the possibility of novel as well as significant developments.

Once again, the insistence of process-thought in inter-relationship as basic to the world should be welcome to Christian theologians. The great biblical affirmations about God are always made with reference to "God-and-his-world." Whatever is said in Scripture about "God-in-himself" is always to be understood as inference from what is known of his activity in creation. And if he is, indeed, what the Christian believes him to be, a loving as well as a living God, then it is obvious that he cannot be seen in abstraction from the world which he loves; for love signifies relationship, and the richest perfection possible is perfection in relationships and not "absolute power" or unchanging substance. An approach to the world and God in terms of process-thought can bring one very close to the Christian conviction that God is genuinely, not simply verbally, describable as "love"--and as love which participates, shares, and even suffers.

The emphasis of process-thinkers on what Whitehead called "the consequent nature" of God--that is to say, on God's being affected by and actually enriched in his activity by that which occurs in his world--can provide some "secular" confirmation for the Christian's conviction that God not only "cares" for the creation but also finds satisfaction in his world. As Hartshorne has insisted, God is not made more divine by that satisfaction, but his deity is given a real enhancement and a genuine delight by what happens in creation; furthermore, the implementation of his purposes is made fuller by these happenings. In other words, the creation matters to him. Contrariwise, failures in the creation and a turning-away from its purpose of augmented good are equally real to God, although in the ongoing process he is able to absorb them into himself and to make them serve his ends in ways which would not otherwise be available.

All this should be of interest to the Christian thinker, for it enables him to find (as we have said) a "secular" confirmation for his belief in the God whose suffering love shares in the world's pain while at the same time his triumphant joy is in part derived from the happiness which the

world can know. The reality of evil and of good, of pain
and of joy, is recognized. But it is seen in relationship to
the basic activity which is God himself who is able both to
bring good out of evil and at the same time to rejoice in the
good which is achieved in the creation. God is vulnerable
and shares the world's pain, yet he can use evil (once it has
occurred) to accomplish good. The Cross, in itself an "evil"
thing, was used by God; and Christians believe it was used
by him to bring about greater good than would have been
possible without it. If at this point they go beyond process-
thought, they do not contradict its insight.

Again, the insistence on the societal nature of the
world, and on man's genuine participation since he himself
is organic to that world, illuminates the Christian belief that
man belongs to the creation and that the whole natural order,
as well as human history and personal experience, is inte-
gral to the purpose of God. This applies both to creation
and to redemption. A false spirituality which would try to
remove man from his material and embodied situation
and regard him as an "angel" is seen for the blatant absurd-
ity which it is; on the other hand, the attempt to think that
God purposes to "save" man out of the world is seen to be
a denial not only of the Christian gospel but of a sound understanding of human nature. Man is a body, as he is a
mind and a spirit. He is, in fact, man; and as man he is
a developing unity in relationship with his fellows, with history, and with nature. Therefore what happens in society,
in the historical process, and in the natural order of events,
has significance for him, because he is participant in this
total pattern. God deals with him in this fashion, not as if
he were an isolated "soul. "

Finally, the stress of process-thought on experience,
and the richness of "presentational immediacy" coupled with
"causal efficacy, " should interest the Christian because it
demonstrates that in what nowadays it is fashionable to call
"meeting, " participation in life, and genuine acquaintance by
sharing, we come to the fullest knowledge both of ourselves
and others and also of the world and God. God is not "up
there" or "out there. " He is here, in the immediacy of our
experience; and it is here that he is to be known, obeyed,
and adored.

Whatever may be said about transcendence must be
said with all this in view. The transcendence of God is his
inexhaustibility, not his remoteness. He is richer and fuller

in his life than any awareness of him which is possible for
us, yet he is not far off but close at hand. He is the "depth"
of things, as he is the "depth" of ourselves; but he is more
than that--he is himself, yet always himself in relation to
that which he is doing, loving, using for the world whose final explanation he is. Even when he is not recognized under some conventional name--even when he is not "named"
at all--he is the inescapable energy which moves through all
things and which works in all things for the richest possible
good. Hence men do not need to be introduced to him as if
they had never met him; what they need is to identify him
where he is, to recognize him as being what he is, and to
see him as doing what he does--which in Christian faith, is
to see him as the dynamic, living, loving "Father of our
Lord Jesus Christ. "

THE DIVINE CALL INTO THE FUTURE*

by John Cobb

Each man's life is oriented around something, or some things. In the immeasurable complexity of his conscious and unconscious experience he attends to some elements and not to others. The language he learns profoundly influences this selectivity of attention, and new modes of attentiveness in their turn influence the language. Of all the words that influence the direction of attention none is more important than "God." The word is indissolubly associated with a claim of importance. If "God" is used, as is so often the case, in association with inherited rules or present mores, attention is focused on them and their claim upon the present. If "God" is used with primary reference to peculiarly religious or mystical elements of experience, attention is focused on them and their claim. If one heeds the claim, one may cultivate, in the first instance, his sensitivity to the implications of the rules or mores; or, in the second instance, the religious or mystical elements of his experience. Such cultivation in the context of this kind of direction of attention is a major aspect of worship. Of course, where "God" is used in these or other ways, he may be rejected, but unless that rejection occurs in the name of "God" understood in another way, it tends to lead to the emptying of experience and life of an integrating orientation and a sense of ultimate importance. This can be avoided only if some other concept, such as nation, justice, freedom, or humanity functions as equivalent to God.

Thus far I have suggested that the serious use of the word "God" plays a major role in the orientation of life and the determination of the elements of experience which gain prominence. If so, the naming as "God" of the One Who Calls us forward has profound importance insofar as it en-

---

courages attention to certain aspects of experience rather
than others. The believer in God so understood attends to
the sensitization of his psychic life to the claim of new possibilities and of his neighbor rather than to inherited rules
or religious feelings. In a community of faith he can improve his capacity to distinguish the call of God from the
myriad other claims arising within and without. The relative weighing of the aspects of his experience is thus altered. One experiences guilt, not in the recognition that his
acts are in conflict with past laws or socially approved patterns, but in the recognition that his bondage to the past and
conformity to human expectations have inhibited his response
to new possibilities of growth and service.

But do not many persons achieve the same result by
rejecting the concept of "God" altogether and orienting their
lives toward ideal ends? Yes, but also, No. Certainly
many who reject "God" are far more sensitive to the call
forward than many who affirm "God." Indeed, as I have
emphasized, "God" has functioned all too much to sanction
what is given and all too little as the One Who Calls. But
if we compare commitment to ideal ends with commitment
to God as the One Who Calls us forward, we can see that
there are inner weaknesses in the idealist's stance which indicate that belief does matter. The one who dedicates himself to ideals does so out of the correct judgment that these
ideals have objectivity to him, that they lay a claim upon
him. Yet he can hardly provide for himself an intelligible
explanation of how this is so. If he rejects God as the
ground of their claim, then he is driven toward describing
them as projections. If one concludes that the value of justice lies not in itself but only in his projection of value upon
it, the intensity of his concern for justice is likely to decline or, at least, to be difficult to communicate to others.
The sense that justice is an inherently worthwhile goal remains, but when it is believed that the value of justice depends solely on the belief that it is valuable, the role of the
sense of its objective value declines. If, on the other hand,
we believe that the claim of justice upon us is an aspect of
the call of God, then our worship of God will include our
sensitization to the importance of that claim and to the concrete relevant possibilities in which the appropriate response
can be embodied.

There is much more that can be said. Apart from
belief in God, conscious or unconscious, there is little
ground for hope. Apart from belief in God, the reason for

concern about one's motives and one's responsibility for them becomes obscure. Apart from belief in God, the claim of the neighbor upon one can only be understood as arbitrary and unfounded. When belief in the God of the Bible is lost, new divinities of the soil, of sexuality, of race and tribe arise and old ones reappear, and the grounds for the prophetic "No!" are gone. Apart from belief in God, history and historical existence become intolerable and barren and we must fall into a pre- or post-historical existence. All this, and more, I believe with respect to the importance of belief, which means, of course, of right belief.

Part III

THEOLOGIES OF THE FUTURE

Study 5

EDWARD SCHILLEBEECKX

CHRISTIAN FAITH IN THE FUTURE

A Theologian for This Season

If it can be said that Pope John's wish to open the windows and let some fresh air into the Church at the Second Vatican Council came true, one of those windows was the Roman Catholic Church of the Netherlands. Among the principal advisors to the Dutch bishops at Vatican II was the Dominican dogmatic theologian, Edward Schillebeeckx. Much of the new "air" that came through the Dutch window was his theological reflection on the sacred and the secular in our time. As he put it in an article written while Vatican II was still in session:

> In our age we have become aware, more than in the past, that our salvation comes about within the one reality that is ours, within the scope of our own life in this world. [1]

Like many Christian theologians of the twentieth century, Schillebeeckx has aimed at overcoming a false distinction between the sacred and the secular. This is one that draws a line of strict separation between the institutional Church with its ceremonies and the world that exists beyond and outside of these solemn occasions. This way of distinguishing the sacred and the secular makes the Church appear as a strange appendage to the structures of the world. It seems to many modern men to be a rather absurd activity on the margin of the world's everyday business. Schillebeeckx, taking his cue from Jesus' preaching of the kingdom of God, has repeatedly argued that Christ himself was, and for believers is still, a sacrament or a bestowal of saving grace by God in and for secular history. [2] Jesus preached the same message whether he was found in the temple at Jerusalem, or in a synagogue of a city or a town, or in an

88

open field or on a sandy beach where men and women were working. All of the institutions of this age, including temple and imperial government, were directed to their final end in the reign of God Himself which would be God's own world-judging, world-redeeming act. The sacred and the secular were therefore both subject to judgment and to the promise of grace. Every deed, every act of men, whether as individuals or as communities, whether performed in the temple or in the market place, would be judged. Cups of cold water given to the thirsty, bread shared with the hungry, ministry to the sick, to prisoners, to widows and orphans would count as acts of worship just as much as almsgiving, or prayer, or fasting.[3] Schillebeeckx called it "secular worship."[4] He also saw it as the practice of life which, when it happens in the world, interprets the dogma of the "kingdom of God" for men and women in a given time and place.[5] Thus the practice of Christian life in the world is for Schillebeeckx the basis for, and not merely the result of, the interpretation of the Bible or of the Church's official teachings. Dogma here does not come before life, but is translated from life to life by Life. The Church bears witness to this process and is itself a sacrament of the grace that has been bestowed for the salvation of the world. As such the Church is "the sacramentum mundi, the 'sign of the world, ' the world itself brought to epiphany."[6]

The views of Edward Schillebeeckx and of many in the Dutch hierarchy whom he has served as professor of dogmatic theology at the University of Nijmegen, Holland, have been matters of controversy in Holland itself and in Rome as well. Schillebeeckx and his colleagues have found themselves in a crossfire between two sorts of criticism. On one side are those who see them as too conservative at heart, erecting a facade of modern thinking for their followers. On the other side are those who see them as radical liberals betraying the essential truth of the faith as they pursue a modern audience. Schillebeeckx has nevertheless been undaunted in his genuine conviction that a person can be at one and the same time a convinced Roman Catholic and a member of the intellectual community of the twentieth century. He understands his task to be the interpretation of Christian dogma for this century and is willing to leave to other theologians of other ages the task of interpreting the apostolic faith for their time.

Schillebeeckx was born in Antwerp, Belgium in 1914. He entered the Dominican Order in 1934. Ordained a priest in 1941, he studied theology at the Sorbonne in Paris where he received the degrees of master and doctor of theology. He taught at an institute of his order in Louvain, Belgium before assuming his chair in dogmatic theology at the University of Nijmegen. He has written many articles and books about the sacraments, secularization, revelation and theological method.[7] He also has been an editor of two Roman Catholic theological journals, one of them the international journal, Concilium. His lecture tour in the United States in early 1968 proved to be as stimulating for the lecturer as for his generally appreciative audiences. This exposure to American pragmatic secular thinking and to American theologians, including the so-called "death-of-God" theologians, William Hamilton and Thomas J. J. Altizer, moved him to engage the issues raised for theology by a modern technological society. His book, God the Future of Man (1968), contains the lectures delivered during his American tour and an "Epilogue: The New Image of God, Secularization and Man's Future on Earth," which was his first theological reflection after his American experience. In his book, God & Man (1969), the concerns stated in the epilogue were more fully developed in a work written as a kind of running dialogue with humanist and Protestant thinkers. The result was a profound articulation of what might best be called a Christian theology of the secular.

NOTES

1. Edward Schillebeeckx, "The Church and Mankind," from The Church and Mankind, Dogma, Vol. I of Concilium (New York: Paulist Press, 1964), p. 69. Reprinted by permission of the publisher.

2. E. Schillebeeckx, Christ the Sacrament of the Encounter with God (New York: Sheed and Ward, 1963), p. 15.

3. See the Gospel according to St. Matthew, Chs. 25:31-46 and 6:1-18.

4. E. Schillebeeckx, "Secular Worship and Church Liturgy," God the Future of Man (New York: Sheed and Ward, 1968), p. 100.

5. Ibid., p. 184f. See text above, p. 12.

6. Ibid., p. 109.

7. Current books in print in English by Schillebeeckx are:
    Church and World. New York: Sheed and Ward,
        1971.
    Layman in the Church. Staten Island, N. Y.: Alva
        House, 1963.
    Celibacy. New York: Sheed and Ward, 1968.
    Christ the Sacrament of the Encounter with God.
        New York: Sheed and Ward, 1963.
    Eucharist. New York: Sheed and Ward, 1968.
    God & Man. New York: Sheed and Ward, 1969.
    Revelation and Theology. 2 vols. New York:
        Sheed and Ward, 1967-68.
    God the Future of Man. New York: Sheed and
        Ward, 1968.
    The Real Achievement of Vatican II. New York:
        Sheed and Ward, 1967.

GOD AS OUR FUTURE*

by Edward Schillebeeckx

As far as man's experience of it and the forms in which it is expressed are concerned, religion is rooted in the culture in which it takes form. In our own period we are seeing the emergence of a new concept of God which is nourished by the cultural soil of our historical situation, within whose structure the whole life of the believer is ordered. Hence the new concept of God is partly determined as to its explicit content and ideas by present-day culture-- a culture not primarily directed towards the past but dynamically orientated towards the future.

Anyone who believes in God and is part of this culture will realize that his faith in God has lost its function as a substitute for human science. He will consequently begin to reflect again and to change his ideas of God. He knows that these are in part historically determined and therefore changeable, and he also knows in advance that even the new ideas that he is seeking will not remain valid forever. But, on the other hand, he knows only too well that his idea of God cannot be relevant to his life if it is entirely at odds with the pattern of his own society and that new ideas of God that are rooted in his own culture will make faith something capable of being experienced by, and of appealing to, modern man, with the result that the Church's confession of God will gain in credibility in the world of today. I should therefore like to give an initial outline of the new concept of God which is now taking shape and in which the believer is trying to express an idea of the living God of "yesterday, today and tomorrow" that will be

---

*From God the Future of Man by E. Schillebeeckx, O. P., © Sheed & Ward Inc., 1968. Reprinted by permission of Sheed & Ward Inc., New York in the United States and possessions, and by permission of Sheed & Ward Limited, London for the British Commonwealth.

grasped and understood today. In doing this, I cannot, of course, go into all the implications of this concept of God.

In the older culture, orientated towards the past, whenever we thought or spoke of God's transcendence we used, almost automatically, to project God into the past. Eternity was rather like an unchangeable and petrified or eternalized "past"--"in the beginning was God. " Men knew very well that God's eternity embraced man's present, past and future and that God was not only "the first, " but also "the last" and therefore the presence whose eternal present transcended our present. The older theology had wonderful things to say about this, things which have in no way lost their value. But in that older civilization in which men's eyes were always turned towards the past, a powerful mutual attraction was felt between "transcendence" and eternity on the one hand and an eternalized "past" on the other. Now, however, in a culture which is resolutely turned towards the future as something that it means to make, what has in fact come about is that the flexible Christian concept of "transcendence, " which is open to more than one meaning, is also affected by this shift. "Transcendence" thus tends to acquire a special affinity with what is called in our temporality "future. " For, if divine transcendence really transcends and embraces, from within, man's past, present and future, the believer will choose, as soon as man has come to recognize the primacy of the future in temporality, to associate God's transcendence with the future, and he will be right in doing this. He will associate God with man's future, and since this individual person lives within a community of persons, he will eventually also associate God with the future of mankind as a whole. This, then, is the real seed ground for the new image of God in our new culture-- provided, of course, that the reality of true faith in the invisible God who is the source of the movement impelling man to "form a concept" of God in the light of his worldly experience has been accepted.

In such a cultural framework, the God of those who believe in him will obviously reveal himself as the "one who is to come, " the God who is our future. This, of course, brings about a radical change--the God whom we formerly, in the light of an earlier view of man and the world, called the "wholly Other" now manifests himself as the "wholly New, " the One who is our future, who creates the future of mankind anew. He shows himself as the God who gives us in Jesus Christ the possibility of making the future--that is, of making everything new and transcending our sinful past and that of all men. The new culture thus becomes the point of departure for the surprising rediscovery of the fact that the God of the promise again gives us the task of setting out towards the promised land, a land that we ourselves, trusting in the promise, must reclaim and cultivate, as Israel did in the past.

A faith in God as the One who is to come, as the future of the individual person and the community of persons, must show its effectiveness in and to this world if it is to avoid being dismissed as incredible because of the preunderstanding of our contemporaries. Faith which has as its content the divine promise of an ultimate eschatological fulfillment for every man and in every moment of our lives proclaims God as the One who is to come--and, what is more, as the One who is to come in the very history that he nonetheless transcends--has to do this precisely by making this history new. Believers themselves will have to show, in their total commitment to life, where the richest springs are that can overcome the evil that deprives man of his joy and improve the world by really caring for man. In their total commitment, they will have to show who they are and who have the power to protect the constantly threatened dignity of man and to bring salvation here and now. At this level, faith in God as the future for man and mankind will have to prove itself true.

Of course, this new concept of God implies a criticism of the earlier idea of God and of the concrete practice of Christian life that resulted from that idea of God. Anyone whose entire being is, culturally and religiously, orientated towards the past inevitably runs the risk of leaving the world as it is, of interpreting it, but not changing it-- this was Karl Marx's legitimate criticism of the religion of his time. This attitude also runs the risk of by-passing the terrestrial future and taking hold of the post-terrestrial future directly. In our new culture, however, Christian faith in a post-terrestrial future can only be seen to be true if this eschatological hope shows itself capable of bringing mankind to a better future here and now. Who could believe in a God who will make everything new "later" if it is in no way apparent from the activity of those who hope in the One who is to come that he is already beginning to make everything new now--if in fact it is not apparent that this eschatological hope is able now to change the course of history for the better? Christian commitment to the world by concern for man will therefore be the exegesis or hermeneutics of the new concept of God, in which God is really shown to be the "wholly New One. " It will have to be clear from the concrete practice of Christian life that God de facto manifests himself as the one whose power can bring about the new future.

It is only from the vantage-point of this exegesis of the new concept of God in and through total Christian commitment to life that we shall, in the second place, be able to reconsider the past so as to interpret or reinterpret it. In so doing, we shall understand how the earlier Christian experience of God was, in an older civilization, justified, but is nonetheless subject to the criticism of the biblical "God of promise" whom we have been permitted to rediscover as a result of the cultural change of today. The identity of the new concept of God with the original Christian message will have to come indirectly to light in the activity of Christians themselves. If a reinterpretation of the Christian message produces an activity in which its identity with the gospel cannot be discovered, this interpretation cannot be a Christian interpretation. It will therefore be apparent that there is a special kind of understanding which is appropriate to statements about faith--such statements, after all, have nothing to do with ideology. Hermeneutics consisting of the very practice of Christian life are therefore the basis for the concrete exegesis of ancient, biblical or magisterial texts.

The distinctive contribution that eschatological hope can make to truly human progress in the world for the salvation of all men itself interprets the dogma of the "kingdom of God, " in which "neither shall there be mourning nor crying nor pain any more" (Rev. 21:4). "According to his promise we wait for new heavens and a new earth in which righteousness dwells" (II Peter 3:13). This goal of Christian hope seems to have a positive content. It is certainly positive in its suggestive power, but on closer inspection it is first and foremost a powerful "symbol that makes us think, " a call to us to transcend what we have made--war, injustice, the absence of peace, the absence of love. We have, however, also been promised, in an example or prototype, that all this will pass away--the historical act of the man Jesus Christ and God's setting of his seal on this life by what we, in faith, call "resurrection. " This reality is the most powerful religious symbol of what is truly possible as the future, the future which has de facto already commenced in Jesus as the Christ.

In the Bible, the expression "to do the truth" is used for the Christian attitude described. This gives emphasis to a concept of truth clearly different from the western idea of truth that was taken over from Hellenism, an idea which contains a fatal division because of the distinction that it makes, in spite of all the careful shades of meaning with which it is used, between theoretical and practical reason. It is certainly not necessary to accept all the implications of American pragmatism for one to be convinced of the truth of what I often heard at table in the United States--"The proof of the pudding is in the eating. " One has, however, to be on one's guard against a short-circuit that often occurs here in Christian thought. Because God has promised us a future of salvation in grace despite our sinful history, it is easy for us to believe that this future in grace falls vertically into the terrestrial event, which would otherwise simply continue to take place as history without salvation. But eschatological hope implies faith that the Christian, by God's justification, is responsible for the terrestrial event itself becoming a history of salvation. In and through his attitude of faith, then, the Christian is already seeking to overcome all that is opposed to salvation in this world, to resist everything that has made and is still making our history a history without salvation and thus to make salvation triumph more and more. Just as our sinful freedom makes our human history into a history without salvation, so too will God transform this history without salvation into a saving event in and through our freedom into which we have been liberated in faith. The believer not only interprets history--he above all changes it. Anyone who disputes this is clearly forgetting that human freedom is the pivot of the historical event--via human freedom, grace is thus able to change history itself. This was the reason why I believed that it was possible to say that the credibility of the Christian must be indirectly apparent in the practice of Christian life. In our new culture, then, a theological treatise about God will be the culmination and completion of an exegesis which consists in the practice of the Christian life. If this Christian practice is absent, the Christian faith will not be credible to modern man, who is sick of ideology, and is always ready to express the irrefutable reproach, "Words, words, words. "

The new concept of God that is, faith in the One who is to come, in the "wholly New One" who provides us here and now with the possibility of making human events into a history of salvation through an inward re-creation which

makes us "new creatures" dead to sin, thus radically trans-
forms our commitment to make a world more worthy of man,
but at the same time it reduces to only relative value every
result which has so far been achieved. The believer, who
knows of the eschatological fulfillment promised to mankind
and to man's history, will be unable to recognize in anything that has already been accomplished "a new heaven and
a new earth." Unlike the Marxist, for example, he will not
even venture to give a positive name to the ultimate fulfillment that is to come. The Christian leaves the future much
more open than the Marxist; for example, he will not even
venture to give a positive name to the ultimate fulfillment
that is to come. The Christian leaves the future much more
open than the Marxist; in his view, the Marxist tends to
close the possibilities prematurely. For the Christian, it
is an ideological misconception to call one concrete stage in
the development of human history the ultimate point.

It is of course, possible to raise the following objection to what I have said--that it gives rise to a new identification which runs parallel with what has been objected to
in the older experience of faith; in other words, an identification between faith in God and the new culture. In reply
to this, I should like to say that no such identification has
been made--all that I have done is to describe how faith
must function in the new culture. My purpose in this has
been to prevent anyone who is whole-heartedly taking part
in the new culture from letting faith remain an attitude that
cannot be realized, something that alienates him from the
world because it forces him to live in two worlds, the
world of science and technology, in which he carries out his
secular task, and a world of fantasy which he has to enter
in his faith. Objections such as the one expressed above
give the impression that the questioner is of the opinion that
the Christian faith must be made perfectly clear once and
for all. I am unable to agree with this claim. I feel bound
to say only this--that we, as Christians, can only expect to
settle the problems of faith within our own society. Later
generations will have to concern themselves with their own
period, and we cannot anticipate their problems. It is not
possible to provide a justification of the Christian faith that
will be valid for all time, but it is possible to do so for the
period in which we are living. The Christian authenticity of
our present culture differs from that of other cultures,
whether those which have become obsolete or those which
may perhaps take form later on. Everyone must achieve
Christian authenticity within the form of his own culture.

It is still possible to go further with the objection to my argument and, although agreeing that no new identification has been made, say that this "new" God, known as the "power of the future," is surely a new projection. The only reply that I can make to this is that this same objection can be made to every religious faith and to every concept of God, whether it is new or old or still in the distant future. But this is not under discussion here. All that I am concerned with is to examine how the believer in God, for whom God is not a projection, can express his profession of faith in God in the new culture--this, at least, is what I have had in mind in writing this particular article. In the light of this newly thematized faith, a fruitful dialogue can once again be opened with atheism and secularism. If we believers do not reinterpret our concept of God, the dialogue will to a very great extent be factually concerned with the different cultural worlds that the partners inhabit. The inevitable consequence of this will be that the perspective of both the believer and the unbeliever will be distorted at the very outset of the dialogue, since when the believer talks about religion, he will be understood by the unbelieving partner as talking about a (past) culture.

On the other hand one should not forget the biblical basis of this so-called new idea of God. The new culture was only the occasion for our rediscovery, especially in the Old Testament, of the living God as "our future." Neither should one overlook the fact that, according to the Bible, the foundation of the eschatological expectation is the certainty in faith of communion with God here and now. When the Bible posits the primacy of the future, it does not intend to deny man's present communication with the God of the Covenant. The foundation of hope is faith in Yahweh who reveals himself as the living God of the community. The neglect of this biblical foundation is an unmistakable drawback in some of the recent "theologies of hope." This neglect fosters an unjustified identification of the promotion of the well-being of all people with the coming kingdom of God.

Moreover, for Christianity the foundation, norm and criterion of every future expectation is its relationship with the past, i. e. with Jesus of Nazareth and what has taken place in him. The Church of Christ is prophetic, but only on the basis of her faith that Jesus is the Christ. The Lord is prior to every Christian community, and for that reason the "saving past" of Jesus, as it is relived in the preaching of the Church, implies a criticism of the religious interpretations of contemporary Christianity. Even for Jesus himself the direct relationship with God, whom he calls his Father, is the basis of his conception of the coming kingdom of God (E. Käsemann). Without this attention to the present relationship with God and to Jesus' past, which the Spirit "brings to our remembrance," even the new idea of God appears to be in danger of becoming a new mythology.

On the basis of the new concept of God which, in keeping with the Old and New Testaments, involves the believer fully in the world in which human history is taking place here and now and in which our Christian freedom, liberated in faith, has to transform man's opposition to salvation into salvation, it is indeed possible to speak of a total secularization, but of a secularization in a theological sense, not in the pseudo-Christian sense which eliminates the reality of God--omits it or simply does not discuss it at all. It is a question of secularization in the theological sense-- in other words, of an attitude which recognizes the presence of God in our human history and which can help to bring about a future of salvation for all men by concern for our fellow-men. It is an attitude in which we, recognizing God in the man Jesus, also recognize him in our fellow-man, who call us to the love which seeks justice for all men. Our faith in God will then become "secular"; in other words, it will assume the form of a love of man which is opposed to history without salvation and which strives to transform the concrete reality in which we are placed into a history of salvation for all men. God does not therefore disappear-- on the contrary, he will begin to penetrate the whole of our life on this earth. He will, it is true, not be so tangible as he was in a religious attitude which reserved one half of life for purely secular activities and the other for religious practices (a form of schizophrenia which even in the past was never recognized by genuine Christians!) Rather, he will appear in the guise of a servant who is entirely at the disposal of his fellow-man. Apparently absent, he will thus, because of his all-penetrating immediacy, be more intimately close to us. Religious man sees himself confronted with the task of committing himself heart and soul to the future history of mankind in the light of his faith in the God who is to come. In this, we shall hasten his final coming which is really nothing but the other side of his coming in grace itself, since his coming always runs ahead of our efforts. That is the paradox of Christianity--we tread in the footsteps of the God who is to come to us from the future and, in so doing, it is still we who make history.

JÜRGEN MOLTMANN

VISION OF HOPE

A Protestant Perspective

In his 1535 "Lectures on Galatians" Martin Luther contemplated the difference between "faith" and "hope. " He was quite sure that in reality one cannot really separate faith from hope. Where one exists, the other is present also. But he believed that it is quite possible to distinguish between them in terms of their respective functions and aims in the life of the believer. According to Luther:

> ... faith commands and directs the intellect, though not apart from the will, and teaches what must be believed. Therefore faith is teaching or knowledge. Hope is exhortation, because it arouses the mind to be brave and resolute, so that it dares, endures and lasts in the midst of evils and looks for better things. Furthermore, faith is a theologian and a judge, battling against errors and heresies, and judging spirits and doctrines. On the other hand, hope is a captain, battling against feelings such as tribulation, despair, and blasphemy; and it battles with joy and courage, etc., in opposition to those great evils. Finally, they differ in their objects. As its object faith has truth, and it teaches us to cling to this surely and firmly; it looks to the word of the object, that is, to the promise. Hope has goodness as its object; and it looks to the object of the word, that is, to the thing promised or the things to be hoped for, which faith has ordered us to accept.[1]

In his work, Theology of Hope, Jürgen Moltmann has illuminated a much neglected dimension of the Christian

life--namely, the ultimate, or final hope of the Christian
Church as expressed in the picture of Jesus Christ coming
in the end to judge both the quick and the dead. Moltmann's
work has proved to be a necessary corrective to the tendency among Protestant theologians to focus on the relationship
between doctrine and faith to the exclusion of the Christian
life. The result has been an unfortunate divorce of theology from concrete life. Moltmann is in a revolt against a
theology of "faith" that is oriented to the past in such a way
that its moral implication is to preserve the status quo of
the institutions of society. His basic concern is to promote
a theology of the future which would call into question all
injustice in the present and would be actively engaged in the
task of creating more humane structures for the people of
the world who would be united by a common future. Far
from being deterred by the caveats of many contemporary
philosophers and politicians against utopian thinking, Moltmann has frankly embraced it in the name of a theology of
hope. It should not come to the reader as a surprise,
therefore, that Moltmann has been one of the leaders in
calling for a dialogue between Christians and Marxists. In
common cause with Marxist goals for society, Moltmann
has called for more than revolution that can spill back on
men in the form of political reaction. He has called for a
"provolution, " a thrust of mankind to a whole new stage of
life where all economic misery and all political alienation
is overcome.[2] The relation between faith and hope as conceived by Luther has been entirely reversed in Moltmann's
theological program. Hope sets the agenda and faith works
for it.

Whether this reversal of the roles of faith and hope
can be justified is the basic issue between Moltmann and his
critics. The chief warrant for hope in a whole new future
for human life is found by Moltmann in the New Testament
portrayal of Jesus as one who came announcing the end of
this age and the approach of the kingdom of God. The
Christian hope in a new heaven and a new earth is claimed
by Moltmann as the reason to hope for a qualitatively new
future on earth. Just as Teilhard de Chardin linked the
Christian doctrine of last things with a final stage of human
evolution, Moltmann has linked it with the historical aims
of dialectical materialism. While appreciative of the emphases of evolutionary theology and process theology on the
appearance of new forms and new stages of life, Moltmann
has kept his distance from the metaphysical theories of
these theologies. He prefers to stay with the vivid language

of the Bible so that, like Jesus, he may bring a word of
judgment and grace on the minions of the market place and
on political officials reaping rewards from injustice. As
long as there are theologians who will use Christian theology to rationalize and defend present injustices, Moltmann
would demonstrate that Christian theology more readily lends
itself to criticism of present structures and to active support
of those who are politically and ecomonically oppressed.

Jürgen Moltmann is now Professor of Theology in the
Protestant theological faculty at the University at Tuebingen,
Germany, where he received his doctorate. He has taught
at the University at Bonn and was Visiting Professor in Theology at Duke University in North Carolina. His call for a
theology of hope has been favorably received by Roman
Catholic theologians who were working along the same lines
within their own theological heritage. Most notable of these
is Fr. Johannes Metz of the University at Münster in Germany. While it is to be expected that the average American
layman will not be able to muster very much enthusiasm for
a theology which consciously seeks dialogue with Marxism,
he should remember that Moltmann and Metz live in a context where Marxism has become an entrenched reality in the
political landscape. They cannot teach and write as theologians in Europe as if Europe were not divided between capi-
talism and communism. The American reader should also
remember that the dialogue between Christians and Marxists
is not really a new phenomenon in Western Europe. It actually began when Marx himself challenged Christian churches
to consider the poor in their own lands. Many pastors, theologians, and Christian laymen responded to the challenge
and the result was the establishment of a Christian socialist
movement in Germany and Switzerland before World War I.
Today many protestant and Catholic clergy and laity are active supporters of the German Social Democratic Party, the
party of Willi Brandt, which has combined certain elements
of Marxist doctrine with democracy. In circles such as this
the dialogue between Christianity and Marxism is silently
and implicitly carried on, if not always audibly and explicit-
ly. Marx has been the mentor of German intellectuals in
church and society, just as Freud has been for American
intellectuals. Moltmann's Theology of Hope belongs to the
implicit dialogue with Marxism in that it furnishes a Christian understanding of the future which challenges, rather than
ratifies, present structures.

NOTES

1. From Luther's Works, Volume 27, edited by Jaroslav
   Pelikan. Copyright 1964 by Concordia Publishing
   House, St. Louis, Missouri. Used by permission.

2. Jürgen Moltmann, "Religion, Revolution, and the Future,"
   The Future of Hope (Philadelphia: Fortress Press,
   1971), p. 126. This essay is now included in a
   book by Moltmann, Religion, Revolution and the Future (New York: Charles Scribner's Sons, 1969).

THE GOSPEL AS HOPE IN HISTORY*

by Jürgen Moltmann

Israel's Experience of History

Beneath the star of the promise of God it becomes possible to experience reality as "history." The stage for what can be experienced, remembered and expected as "history" is set and filled, revealed and fashioned, by promise.

The promises of God disclose the horizons of history--whereby "horizon," as it is aptly put by H. G. Gadamer, is not to be understood as "a rigid boundary," but as "a thing towards which we are moving, and which moves along with us." Israel lived within these moving horizons of promise and experienced reality within the fields of tension they involve. Even when the period of nomadic wanderings ended in Palestine, this mode of experiencing, remembering and expecting reality as history still remained and characterized this people's wholly peculiar relation to time. The realm of Palestinian culture did not turn time for them into a figure of cyclic recurrence, but on the contrary, a historic experience of time repeatedly asserted itself prevailingly over an unhistoric experience of space and turned the occupied areas of the land into temporal periods of an all-embracing history.

What could here be experienced as "history" in the potential changes of reality always reached as far as the promises of God stretched men's memories and expectations. "Israel's history existed only in so far as God accompanied her, and it is only this time-span which can properly be de-

scribed as her history. " This fact of God's accompanying
his people, however, was always seen within the area of
tension between a manifest promise on the one hand and the
expected redeeming of this promise on the other. It was
within the span of this tension that history became of interest to Israel. "Only where Yahweh had·revealed himself in
his word and acts did history exist for Israel. " This means,
however, that the experience of reality as history was made
possible for Israel by the fact that God was revealed to Israel in his promises and that Israel saw the revealing of
God again and again in the uttering of his promises.

Now, if events are thus experienced within the horizon of remembered and expected promises, then they are
experienced as truly "historic" events. They do not then
have only the accidental, individual and relative character
which we normally ascribed to historic events, but then they
have always at the same time also an unfinished and provisional character that points forwards. Not only words of
promise, but also the events themselves, in so far as they
are experienced as "historic" events within the horizon of
promise and hope, bear the mask of something that is still
outstanding, not yet finalized, not yet realized. "Here everything is in motion, the accounts never balance, and fulfillment unexpectedly gives rise in turn to another promise
of something greater still. Here nothing has its ultimate
meaning in itself, but is always an earnest of something
still greater. " The overspill of promise means that the
facts of history can never be regarded as processes complete in themselves which have had their day and can manifest their own truth by themselves. They must be understood as stages on a road that goes further and elements in
a process that continues. Hence the events that are "historically" remembered in this way do not yet have their ultimate truth in themselves, but receive it only from the
goal that has been promised by God and is to be expected
from him. Then, however, the events that are thus experienced as 'historic' events give a foretaste of the promised
future. The overspill of promise means that they have always a provisional character. They contain the note of
"provisio, " i. e. , they intimate and point forward to something which does not yet exist in its fullness in them.
Hence the history that is thus experienced and transmitted
forces every new present to analysis and to interpretation.
Events that have been experienced in this way 'must' be
passed on, because in them something is seen which is determinative also for future generations. They cast their

shadow, or shed their light, on the way ahead. On the other hand they may also be freely interpreted and actualized by each new present, since they are never so firmly established that we could restrict ourselves merely to ascertaining what they once were.

The ancient historic traditions give expression to experiences which Israel had of its God and his promises. But if these promises reach out into that future which is still ahead of the present, then the historic narratives concerned cannot merely narrate experiences of the past. Rather, the whole narrative and representation of this past will lead us to open ourselves and our present to that same future. The reality of history is narrated within the horizon of the history of the working of God's promises. The stories of Israelite history--the histories of the patriarchs, of the wilderness, of David--are treated as themes pregnant with future.

Even where the historic tradition passes over into legendary tradition, the peculiarly Israelite tradition is still dominated by the hopes and expectations kindled by Yahweh's promises. Since the history that was once experienced contains an element that transcends history in its pastness and is pregnant with future, and to the extent that this is so, two things follow: first, this history must again and again be recalled and brought to mind in the present, and secondly, it must be so expounded to the present that the latter can derive from history an understanding of itself and its future path and can also find its own place in the history of the working of God's promises.

The peculiarity of Israelite accounts of history as "historiography conditioned by faith in the promise" is particularly outstanding in comparison with the accounts of history in other peoples and other religions. "In the Greek and Roman mythologies, the past is re-presented as an everlasting foundation. In the Hebrew and Christian view of history the past is a promise to the future; consequently, the interpretation of the past becomes a prophecy in reverse. "

The history of Israel shows again and again that the promises to which Israel owes its existence prove amid all the upheavals of history to be a continuum in which Israel was able to recognize the faithfulness of its God. It could perhaps be said that the promises enter into fulfillment in events, yet are not completely resolved in any event, but there remains an overspill that points to the future. That is why reality, as it comes and is awaited and as it passes and is left behind, is experienced as history, and not as a cosmic and ever-recurring constant. It is experienced not in the epiphany of the eternal present, but in expectation of the manifestation and fulfillment of a promised future.

That is why the present itself, too, is not the present of the Absolute--a present with which and in which we could abide--but is, so to speak, the advancing front line of time as directed purposefully towards its goal in the moving horizon of promise. If the promise of God is the condition on which it becomes possible to have historic experience of reality, then the language of historic facts is the language of promise--otherwise events can be called neither "historic" nor "eloquent." The promises of God initiate history for Israel and retain the control in all historic experience.

If we are prepared to understand divine revelation and the knowledge of God within the horizon of history as the sphere of promise, then we shall be able to reach the following conclusions:

1. God reveals himself as "God" where he shows himself as the same and is thus known as the same. He becomes identifiable where he identifies himself with himself in the historic act of his faithfulness. The presupposition for the knowledge of God is the revealing of God by God. To that extent God remains Subject and Lord even of the process of man's knowing. Man's knowing is responsible knowing. But if the revelations of God are promises, then God "himself" is revealed where he "keeps covenant and faithfulness for ever" (Ps. 146:6). Where God, in his faithfulness to a promise he has given, stands to that which he has promised to be, he becomes manifest and knowable as the selfsame Self. "God himself" cannot then be understood as reflection on his transcendent "I-ness," but must be understood as his selfsame-ness in historic faithfulness to his promises.

If God confesses to his covenant and promises in adopting, confirming, renewing, continuing and fulfilling them, then God confesses to God, then he confesses to himself. In proving his faithfulness in history, he reveals himself. For the essence and the identity of the God of promise lies not in his absoluteness over and beyond history, but in the constancy of his freely chosen relation to his creatures, in the constancy of his electing mercy and faithfulness. Hence knowledge of God comes about not in view of a transcendent Super-Ego, not yet in view of the course of an obscure history, but in view of the historic action of God within the horizon of the promises of God. God reveals himself in his name, which discloses the mystery of his Person to the extent that it discloses the mystery of his faithfulness.

The name of God is a name of promise, which promises his presence on the road on which we are set by promise and calling. The name of God and the promises contained in the name of God are therefore not only formulae of self-presentation, but they also tell us something "about" God, for in them he gives surety for his future. They tell us who he will be. They tell us that he will be found on the road his promises point to the future, and where he will be found on that road. That is why the revelation of God and the corresponding knowledge of God are always bound up with the recounting and recalling of history and with prophetic expectation. These two things are not merely developments of his self-revelation, but are obviously a constitutive part of the revelation of his faithfulness and sameness and uniqueness.

Martin Buber has declared: 'It may be claimed to be a fundamental principle of the history of religion that experience of God begins with the experience of a single phenomenon, but knowledge of God begins with the identification of two, i. e. cognition begins with re-cognition." This is to my mind a specifically Old Testament thought. To know God means to re-cognize him. But to re-cognize him is to know him in his historic faithfulness to his promises, to know him therein as the selfsame Self and therefore to know himself. The identifying of two experiences is possible only where there is self-identification, or the revelation of historic faithfulness, because this God guarantees his promises by his name.

2. If knowledge of God is a re-cognizing of God, because revelation of God means that God confesses to God in historic faithfulness to his promises, then it can hardly be said that the historic complex of particular historic events "itself" reveals God. But the history of promise, i. e. the history initiated by promise and covenant and expected as a result of them, does reveal the faithfulness of God to the extent that in it he keeps faith with his promises

and thereby remains true to himself. God is not first known at the end of history, but in the midst of history while it is in the making, remains open and depends upon the play of the promises. That is why this knowledge must constantly remain mindful of the promises that have been issued and of the past exercise of God's faithfulness, and at the same time be a peculiarly hopeful knowledge.

It must be a knowledge that does not merely reflect past history--as a mental picture of completed facts of history--but it must be an interested knowledge, a practical knowledge, a knowledge that is upheld by confidence in the promised faithfulness of God. To know God is to suffer God, says an old adage. But to suffer means to be changed and transformed. Knowledge of God is then an anticipatory knowledge of the future of God, a knowledge of the faithfulness of God which is upheld by the hopes that are called to life by his promises. Knowledge of God is then a knowledge that draws us onwards--not upwards--into situations that are not yet finalized but still outstanding. It is a knowledge not of the looks of past history, but of the outlooks involved in the past promises and past faithfulness of God. Knowledge of God will then anticipate the promised future of God in constant remembrance of the past emergence of God's election, his covenant, his promises and his faithfulness. It is a knowledge that oversteps our bounds and moves within the horizon of remembrance and expectation opened up by the promise, for to know about God is always at the same time to know ourselves called in history by God.

Gospel and Promise

When we come to the question of the view of the revelation of God in the New Testament, then we discover the fact, already familiar from the Old Testament, that there is no unequivocal concept of revelation. What the New Testament understands by revelation is thus again not to be learned from the original content of the words employed, but only from the event to which they are applied. The event to which the New Testament applies the expressions for revelation imparts to them a peculiar dynamic which is messianic in kind and implies a history of promise. The general impression could be described in the first instance by saying that with the cross and resurrection of Christ the one revelation of God, the glory of his lordship which embraces righteousness, life and freedom, has begun to move towards man. In the gospel of the event of Christ this future is already present in the promises of Christ. It proclaims the present breaking-in of this future, and thus vice versa this future announces itself in the promises of the gospel. The proclamation of Christ thus places men in the midst of an event of revelation which embraces the nearness of the coming Lord. It thereby makes the reality of man 'historic' and stakes it on history.

If we now ask what the future of the risen Christ contains by way of promise and expectation, then we discover promises whose content is already lit up in certain outline by the prophetic expectations of the Old Testament, but whose form is determined by the words, the suffering and the death of Christ. The future of Christ which is to be expected can be stated only in promises which bring out and make clear in the form of foreshadowing and prefigurement what is hidden and prepared in him and his history. In this case, too, promise stands between knowing and not knowing, between necessity and possibility, between that which is not yet and that which already is.

The knowledge of the future which is kindled by promise is therefore a knowledge in hope, is therefore prospective and anticipatory, but is therefore also provisional, fragmentary, open, straining beyond itself. It knows the future in striving to bring out the tendencies and latencies of the Christ event of the crucifixion and resurrection, and in seeking to estimate the possibilities opened up by this event. Here the Easter appearances of the crucified Christ are a constant incitement to the consciousness that hopes and anticipates, but on the other hand also suffers and is critical of existence. For these "appearances" make visible something of the eschatological future of the Christ event, and therefore cause us to seek and search for the future revelation of this event. Thus knowledge of Christ becomes anticipatory, provisional and fragmentary knowledge of his future, namely, of what he will be. All the titles of Christ point messianically forward in this sense. On the other hand, knowledge of the future has its stimulus nowhere else than in the riddle of Jesus of Nazareth. It will thus be knowledge of Christ in the urge to know who he is and what is hidden and prepared in him.

Christian eschatology speaks of "Christ and his future. " Its language is the language of promises. It understands history as the reality instituted by promise. In the light of the present promise and hope, the as yet unrealized future of the promise stands in contradiction to given reality. The historic character of reality is experienced in this contradiction, in the front line between ultimate possibilities and dangers is revealed in the event of promise constituted by the resurrection and cross of Christ. We took the promise contained in this event, in the sense of that which is latent, hidden, prepared and intended in this event, and expounded it against the background of the Old Testament history of promise, perceiving at the same the tendencies of the Spirit which arise from these insights. The promissio of the universal future leads of necessity to the universal missio of the Church to all nations.

The promise of divine righteousness in the event of the justification of the godless leads immediately to the hunger for divine right in the godless world, and thus to the struggle for public bodily obedience. The promise of the resurrection of the dead leads at once to love for the true life of the whole imperilled and impaired creation. In expounding the promises in the Christ event in terms of latency and tendency, we discovered a historic process of mediation between subject and object, which allows us neither to assign the future of Christ to a place within some system of world history and of the history of salvation, and thereby make this event relative to something that is foreign to it, acquired from other experiences and imposed upon it from without, nor yet to reflect the future of Christ into the existentialistic futurity of man. The history of the future of Christ and the historic character of the witnesses and missionaries condition each other and stand in a correlation of promissio and missio. The Christian consciousness of history is a consciousness of mission, and only to that extent is it also a consciousness of world history and of the historic character of existence. The mission on which the man of hope is sent into this advance area of universal possibilities pursues the direction of the tendency of God's own action in omnipotently pursuing his faithfulness and his promise. The man of hope who leaves behind the corrupt reality and launches out on to the sea of divine possibilities, thereby radically sets this reality of his at stake--staking it on the hope that the promise of God will win the day.

When we speak of the "future of Jesus Christ, " then we mean that which is described elsewhere as the "parousia of Christ" or the "return of Christ. " Parousia actually does not mean the return of someone who has departed, but "im-

minent arrival. " Parousia can also mean presence, yet not
a presence which is past tomorrow, but a presence which
must be awaited today and tomorrow.   It is the "presence
of what is coming towards us, so to speak an arriving future. " The parousia of Christ is a different thing from a
reality that is experienced now and given now.   As com-
pared with what can now be experienced, it brings something new.   Yet it is not for that reason totally separate
from the reality which we can now experience and have now
to live in, but, as the future that is really outstanding, it
works upon the present by awaking hopes and establishing
resistance.   The eschaton of the parousia of Christ, as a
result of its eschatological promise, causes the present that
can be experienced at any given moment to become historic
by breaking away from the past and breaking out towards the
things that are to come.

Thus we must expect something new from the future.
But if this future is expected as the "future of Jesus Christ, "
then it is not expected from someone new or from someone
else.   What the future is bringing is something which,
through the Christ event of the raising of the one who was
crucified, has become "once and for all" a possible object
of confident hope.   Faith in Jesus as the Christ is not the
end of hope, but it is the confidence in which we hope (Heb.
11:1).   Faith in Christ is the prior of the two, but in this
faith hope has the primacy.

Part IV

THEOLOGIES OF THE HISTORICAL PRESENT

Study 7

HENRY CADE

RADICAL CHRISTIANITY AS BLACK THEOLOGY

The "Black Now"

The "black now" is the historical present, or, to
put it more precisely, the historical present in America is
black. It is the "now" of black consciousness swirling like
a storm through American society, making itself known,
making itself felt and feared. Black consciousness is the
awareness of black people that they must take their identity
from a history of oppression and degradation, from a history of being treated as things, chattels, subhumans, and
in this way seek their authentic humanity. This aspiration,
this truly human and truly dramatic response, this taking
hold of the history of reproach and making it into a story of
glory lies at the heart of what is called "the black revolution. " It is the essence of blackness in the historical present. It is something that only black men and women can
do. Whites, however, can become witnesses of it--witness
in joy or in fear, depending on whether or not they stand in
a repentent relation to the history of the oppression of black
people by whites.

The "black now" is a post-World War II phenomenon.
It is the appearance in these years of the consciousness that
the time has come for the oppression to end. It is the
shared conviction of a community that in their lifetime black
boys and girls will no longer be psychologically distorted
and maimed by racist social structures which say "No!" to
black expectations while fostering white ones. Black theology is a radical Christian response to the demands of the
"black now. " It is a Christian reflection on the black experience by those who know it first hand, by those who live
it every day of their lives. It is the articulation in thought
of those people who refuse to expel either Christ or blackness from their soul, but who hold both together in their
identification with Christ and with one another.

114

Radical Christianity is the faith response of those people who identify with Christianity while at the very same time recognizing that Christianity itself not only is changing, but needs changing. Black theology is an expression of radical Christianity, understood in this way. It should not be confused, however, with the radical Christianity of the so-called "death-of-God" Protestants.[1] Black theology is Christian because it celebrates a living God and a living Christ; it is radical because it calls for the revolutionary overthrow of the dogmas of the traditional Church as well as its institutions. In the contemporary explosion of theology it is probably the most volatile element.

In sharp contradistinction to most of the other Christian theologies represented in this volume, black theology is self-consciously a theology of the historical present, and it looks askance at those theologies which depend on the future to disclose the essential truth of the Christian faith. Convinced that black Christians were led astray in the past and kept subservient by the white man's preaching of heaven as the "golden age to come," black theologians have rejected the traditional doctrine of eschatology. They find essential Christianity not in a teaching about a future heaven and hell, but rather in the message of Jesus Christ to the poor, to the persecuted, to the downtrodden of this world as expressed in his sayings and parables. The kingdom of God, his reign, breaks in now whenever in that "now" the downtrodden receive the message of liberation--namely, "... if the Son makes you free, you will be free indeed" (Jn. 8:36). For black theologians it is the Christian gospel manifesting itself from the center of the "black now." Christian faith is, in their view, radical obedience to the word that appears from Christ in the black here and now. The theological task that follows from it is to reinterpret in the light of this word, and to change where necessary, the doctrines of traditional "white" Christianity.

Black theology is self-conscious in a way that makes it possible for it to be clearly distinguished from Protestant liberal theology, with which it shares many areas of agreement. It is unabashedly Christ-centered, claiming Jesus as "the Black Messiah."[2] It displays a strength of conviction, a passionate commitment to Christ and his Church, the community of the downtrodden, which it finds noticeably lacking in white liberal Christians. Black theology understands itself as articulating the religious basis of black solidarity, the phenomenon which tends to intimidate white people. In the presence of fragmented and atomized whites, black Christians declare their oneness with all of the black peoples of the world. This is no easy task, because many blacks, especially respected black intellectuals, have either renounced or declared their immunity from Christianity on the grounds that it is the white man's instrument of repression.

Just as European theologians responded several generations ago to the challenges of Friedrich Nietzsche, Karl Marx and Ludwig Feuerbach, so black Christian theologians today are responding to the thought of Malcolm X, Eldridge Cleaver, and James Baldwin. Black theologians repeatedly declare their appreciation for the role of these men in evoking a sense of dignity and worth in black people, and the theologians also stress their oneness with them in working for total black liberation. But as black Christians they supply a theological rationale for the struggle that is not necessarily appreciated by the black intellectuals. For example, while Albert Cleage says, "As black preachers we must tell our people that we are God's chosen people and that God is fighting with us as we fight,"[3] Eldridge Cleaver refuses to accept a religious rationale for the struggle for black liberation. In his work, Soul On Ice, he wrote:

> ... not too long ago it was my way of life to preach, as ardently as I could, that the white race is a race of devils, created by their maker to do evil, and make evil appear as good; that the white race is the natural, unchangeable enemy of the black man, who is the original man, owner, maker, cream of the planet Earth; that the white race was soon to be destroyed by Allah, and that the black man would then inherit the earth, which has always, in fact been his.
>
> I have, so to speak, washed my hands in the blood of the martyr, Malcolm X, whose retreat from the precipice of madness created new room for others to turn about in, and I am now caught up in that tiny space, attempting a maneuver of my own. Having renounced the teaching of Elijah Muhammed, I find that a rebirth does not follow automatically of its own accord, that a void is left in one's vision, and this void seeks constantly to obliterate itself by pulling one back to one's former outlook. I have tried a tentative compromise by adopting a

select vocabulary, so that now when I see the
whites of their eyes, instead of saying 'devil' or
'beast, ' I say 'imperialist' or 'colonialist' and everyone seems happier. [4]

If Cleaver has thus rejected the idea of a cosmic struggle in
Black Muslim terms, he would hardly be open to such an
idea in the language of Christianity. So the Black Christian
as Christian cannot assume that he will be any less the subject of reproach and derision than any other witness to
Christ in any other time or place.

A more specific challenge to black theology comes
from the pen of James Baldwin. In his play, Blues for Mr.
Charlie, Lorenzo, a young militant black, condems Christianity as the religion of white racism. Speaking in a church
to its pastor and to the grandmother of a black youth slain
by whites, Lorenzo says:

> ... I wish to God I was in an arsenal. I'm sorry
> Meridian, Mother Henry, I don't mean that for
> you....
>
> ... it was your grandson, Mother Henry, that got
> killed ... just last week, and yet, here you sit in
> this house of this damn almighty God who don't
> care what happens to nobody, unless of course,
> they're white. Mother Henry, I got a lot of respect for you and all that, and for Meridian, too,
> but that white man's god is white. It's that damn
> white God that's been lynching us and burning us
> and castrating us and raping our women and robbing us of everything that makes a man a man for
> all these hundred of years. Now, why we sitting
> around here, in His house? If I could get my
> hands on Him, I'd pull Him out of heaven and drag
> Him through this town at the end of a rope. [5]

It is writing such as this that has radicalized many black
pastors and theologians. They will identify with Christianity
and assume with that the true scandal of faith in Jesus
Christ, but they will reject those doctrines and teachings
which support white racism. To many white observers black
theology and black Christianity are contradictions in terms.
They see it as an identification of the universality of the gospel with the particularity of skin pigmentation. The black
theologian James Cone and Henry Cade, pastor of Central

Presbyterian Church in Newark, have headed off such criticism by pointing to the fact that "black" does not simply
mean skin color, but rather the experience of an oppressed
people. [6] Failure to identify with oppressed blacks is, in
their view, the same sort of failure indicated by Jesus when
he said, "I was hungry and you gave me no food, I was
thirsty and you gave me no drink, I was a stranger and you
did not welcome me, naked and you did not clothe me, sick
and in prison and you did not visit me. "[7] Implicit in the
black theology of James Cone and of Henry Cade is the further statement, "I was black and you did not lift the burden
of oppression. "

Henry Cade, the author of the following selection, was
born in Selma, Alabama. Reared in the South, he attended
Knoxville College, where he received the B. A. degree. He
pursued his theological education at Pittsburgh Theological
Seminary and after graduation served churches in the South
before accepting the call to serve as pastor of Central United Presbyterian Church in downtown Newark. His is a theology forged in the crucible of everyday life in Newark. It
speaks for itself.

NOTES

1. William Hamilton and Thomas J. J. Altizer have iden-
    tified themselves as "death-of-God Protestants" in
    their book Radical Theology and the Death of God
    (New York: Bobbs-Merrill Co., 1966).

2. See Albert E. Cleage, Jr., The Black Messiah (New
    York: Sheed & Ward, 1969), pp. 24-28.

3. Ibid., p. 6.

4. Eldridge Cleaver, Soul On Ice (New York: Dell Pub-
    lishing Co., 1968), p. 66. Used with permission
    of McGraw-Hill Book Company; and Jonathan Cape
    Ltd for British Commonwealth & Empire.

5. James Baldwin, Blues for Mr. Charlie (New York: Dell
    Publishing Co., 1964), p. 15. Used by permission
    of the Dial Press and James Baldwin.

6. James Cone, Black Theology and Black Power (New
    York: Seabury Press, 1969), p. 69, and Henry

Cade, below p. 123f.

7.   Matthew 25:42-43.

THE NEWLY EMERGING BLACK CHURCH*

by Henry Cade

In his book The Secular City, Harvey Cox illustrated his understanding of the eschatological community with a reference to a model city built by the Communists in Poland after they came into power in 1945. Called Nova Huta (New City), it was to be a true sign of the fulfillment of history as expected by Communism. The layout of the city with its many parks, sport stadium and cultural facilities, the government buildings and the domiciles--even the people selected to live there--were all part of the design for a model human community.[1] Here I want to consider "The Newly Emerging Black Church" as the community hopefully which will be in the Christian context "The Nova Huta, " a model of the kingdom of God and a manifestation of a sign or a clue as to where history is going.

Our thoughts concerning the newly emerging black church will be focused on the urban church with all of its complexities. We are moving rapidly, step by step, toward an urban technological society, the so-called global village, so I suppose that unless someone pushes the wrong button, our urban society will be around for a while. I won't attempt to define an urban society. Come to Newark!

In our discussion of "The Newly Emerging Black Church, " we shall consider 1) The Traditional Black Church and Its Submissive-Survival Motif; and 2) The Renewed Black Church "Coming of Age. " Time is of the essence, so I don't have a third point. We cannot afford too many points of procedure. So much time has passed and so little has happened! However, after considering these two basic points, I would like to raise a serious question concerning "The Black Church's Unique Possibility in Recasting the Human Values of our Civilization. "

---

*First delivered as a lecture to New York Theological Seminary by The Reverend Henry Cade on December 9, 1969.

It should be obvious that the black urban church, as well as the white church (there are two, you know!), is in a state of crisis and is experiencing new birth pangs minute by minute and hour by hour. Consequently, black caucuses which cross every major denominational line, including the Roman Catholic Church, are emerging in an effort to deal with the new concerns of mission and ministry. They are seeking to project and map out a pattern for persons struggling and wrestling with identity, purpose and direction for their lives.

Before we go any further, perhaps it would be in order to point out some of the basic characteristics of the urban black church seeking renewal: (a) decline in church membership and attendance; (b) acute financial needs; (c) lack of sufficient personnel; (d) questions concerning the relevancy of the church in the light of the growing concern for personal and community realization; (e) competition from rising semi-religious groups seeking the attention of newcomers; (f) lack of commitment to, and discipline within, the context of faith as an adequate sphere for creative action; (g) black mobility due to the search for adequate housing and for better education and economic opportunities; (h) the migration to urban centers of blacks who for the most part are unable to identify with the church structures that are found there. These are just some of the factors one must keep in mind as he seeks to play a significant role in the newly emerging black church. But on the other hand, one must also be conscious of the "religious trick bag" or spookism that has dominated the black church.

1) The Traditional Black Church
   and its Submissive-Survival Motif

The submissive-survival motif was not always a dominating feature. It grew out of a false concept of the eschatological community projected by white missionaries and prolonged by the institutionalized de-huminization of blacks by the colonizer (America). The white missionaries with their futuristic eschatology had helped to plant in black spirits the idea of gaining eternal life upon death at the costly expense of an historical earthly damnation. In his Autobiography Malcolm X portrayed in vivid fashion an understanding of this religious trick bag. "The black man in North America was spiritually sick because for centuries he had accepted the white man's Christianity--which asked the black so-called

Christian to expect no true Brotherhood of Man, but to endure the cruelties of the White so-called Christians. Christianity had made black men fuzzy, nebulous, confused in their thinking. It had taught the black man to think if he had no shoes, and was hungry, 'we gonna get shoes and milk and honey, and fish fries in heaven. '"[2] It is interesting to note here that the black church did not always project this kind of false hope.

The pre-Civil-War black church projected a different life style and attitude. Most slaves within their own conscious identities refused to accept the white man's definition of black humanity and so resisted this false identity with every ounce of humanity in them.

Even though the submissive-survival technique was manifested by the slaves, history tells us that they never accepted without question the inhumanity of their colonizers. This is revealed in many historical manifestations: Richard Allen and his group walking out of the white church in 1787; Nat Turner, the Baptist preacher, organizing a slave revolt; the underground railroad; the many freedom songs ("Before I'll be a slave, I'll be buried in my grave and go home to my Lord and be free, " "Go down Moses"); the conflicts between master and slave; and finally slave plots all over the North and South by various black leaders. The point is that the black church was not always engulfed in the submissive-survival motif. This kind of submissive attitude grew later as an unhealthy response to the strange social strategy of the colonizing establishment--America, land of the free and home of the brave!

History tells us that following the Civil War, democracy "of the people, by the people and for the people" was a living reality for about ten or fifteen years. This was when a meaningful number of black and white representatives who were responsible to the people were elected to high government positions. But history reveals another grim lesson! Every time black people begin to take their own cause seriously, this country becomes alarmed and uses its power to stop the flow of black creativity. Consequently, following the reconstruction period, the colonizers began their entrenchment policy of de-humanizing the blacks in their midst. The submissive-survival motif emerged as a way of life. The result is well known: a series of laws that stripped black people of all rights of personality and made color a badge of servitude. A new way of life was estab-

lished on the assumption that black people are hopelessly
ignorant and inferior. Daily reminders of being black and
therefore useless were ingeniously developed for the ongoing social brain-washing of both white and black people in
a segregated society. The dominant impression given was
that being black was a crime and so black existence as such
was a crime against the state. Lynchings, segregation,
burnings, discrimination characterized the climate within
which American facism was born. For black people it meant
a destruction of the human personality--a loss of the sense
of somebodyness. In the process this de-humanizing feature
was sanctified by religion, justified by philosophy, and le-
galized by the Supreme Court--all institutions of the colonizers.

In the sheer effort to survive as a minority in the
midst of a frightened and hostile majority, black people began to assume the role and with that the identity conferred
by the new system. The philosophy of the white mission-
aries--the false futuristic eschatology--began to penetrate
the black church and its ministry. After reconstruction, the
black church became a place of refuge from the racist social structures that replaced slavery. As such it was no
longer a community of protest and liberation. The effectiveness of the brain-washing of the colonizers can be discerned
in the fact that even there in the haven of retreat, the black
church and black minister co-operated with the white system's
de-humanization process. The real sin of the black churches
is revealed in the fact that they convinced themselves of this
false identity.

But now this attitude of accomodation to white racist
structures is coming to an end. As one black writer has
put it, "We must begin to move. The whole black world
must begin to move, though we will not even be able to see
anything concrete for at least five to ten years." While
combating the submissive-survival motif is only a part of the
role of the newly emerging black church, it is of the utmost
importance to begin to move black people (and white as well)
toward a new realization of humanity and civilization. We
cannot begin to move until that submissive attitude is at an end.

2) The Renewed Black Church "Coming of Age":
   Black Theology and The Black Experience

A thirst for human creativity and the collapse of the

traditional black submissive-survival motif are the two main hallmarks of the struggle of the black church. We have seen evidences of the collapse of the submissive-survival motif and its inherent accommodation in every area of black endeavor from sports, business to politics. We are now witnessing the continuing thirst for human creativity which the old black church could scarcely cultivate, much less embody. Consequently, the greatest need for the newly emerging black church is for the awareness of a new self concept. That is why there is an unceasing striving toward personal and community self-determination and self-realization. It is a matter of new wine skins for new wine. Nothing else will do! This means that the newly emerging black church must come to terms with the black revolutionary consciousness, if it is to gain the respect and commitment of followers from the community, if it is to recapture its missionary impact--if it is to be heard again! There are nine features that I have observed personally in the black movement on the urban scene.

The first five features deal with personal development and creativity:

1. Restoration of human respect. Here the emerging black church demonstrates an authentic understanding of sin, guilt, and forgiveness, not in terms of white dehumanization, but rather as the restoration of manhood, personhood, womanhood, which is to say genuine creaturehood. This means a regained sense of somebodyness through faith in the crucified and risen Jesus Christ who has affirmed our basic personhood.

2. Identity: Who am I? This question is answered in terms of basic acceptance, namely--a child of God, one loved by Christ, a member of common humanity with potential for creativity, etc.

3. Strong self concept. Here the black church takes itself seriously again, and so exposes those who do not take themselves seriously because they have been brain-washed by white racists. To believe in ourselves is to forget what others think of us.

4. Purpose. To glorify Christ through our own cultural heritage which is not the European heritage. To be godly, not to be devils, is to relate to life through Christ, neighbor and self, through community and the world!

5. Direction. This is determined in the context of self-analysis as defined by ourselves, not by somebody else.

The last four features are expressions of our self concept and personal creativity within the context of the community:

6. Community determination and realization. Here the black community resolves to play a determinative role in the decision-making process of our socioeconomic and political destiny.

7. Mobilization. This means raising black consciousness, etc.

8. Organization. Here the black church gathers people around vital issues.

9. The ultimate objective. As a movement toward personal and collective spiritual wholeness, it means coming alive and taking our places on the stage of history in the conviction that the Word became flesh and dwelt among us!

These features also inform the new sense of nationalism that is generating a lot of black community organization. Black nationalism is rooted in a black value system and black culture. The black value system is discerned in how one lives, to what end one lives--unity, self-determination. Thus collective work and responsibility, co-operative economics are the primary evidences of the purpose, creativity and faith of the black value system.

Culture is the synthesis of a people's activities. It is that which enables a people to regulate their lives. It furnishes the physical and institutional equipment required for the survival of a people. The black value system and culture both come to expression in nationalism as a philosophy which seeks to promote a positive sense of group consciousness.

The philosophy of nationalism generates the understanding that a people belongs together. It seeks to unify the culture, values and needs of a people. Historically, nationalism has been the means by which an oppressed people achieved liberation and nationhood. Black nationalism, then, is the philosophy which seeks to bind black people together through the creation of a common feeling of group identity or peoplehood. To inspire common orientation and action for liberation against the oppression of the dominant white group.

Economic, political, military and social self-determination are its aims. Community organization is the process through which a community is empowered for the purpose of achieving an active voice in those affairs which affect it and its members. It is the means by which a community may gain a role of power in the decisions concerning its life, its health, its atmosphere--in short, its total well-being.

These are monumental tasks. Nevertheless, if the black church is to witness again, it must accept this agonizing responsibility. At Central United Presbyterian Church of Newark, we are attempting to take our ministry seriously by letting the world write our agenda. We are attempting to move toward the realization of various task groups in the light of various phases of missionary engagement. Our worship services are being designed in this fashion:

> 1st Sunday: The Lord's Supper is celebrated in the light of our missionary engagement. Worship without missionary engagement is invalid. Commitment to Jesus Christ must be realized within the context of our social-economic political environment.

> 2nd Sunday: The focus is on black theology and the black experience. Here the community seeks to relate the Christian faith to black experience.

> 3rd Sunday: Evangelism and youth out-reach.

> 4th Sunday: Emphasizing mission out-reach through task groups. Reports are given during worship, etc.

> 5th Sunday: The role of the Church and community's self-determination.

Our overall purpose is to relate the church to the rising levels of consciousness, of black awareness, and thirst for liberation and nationhood that have come to expression in Newark and in other urban centers. We have recognized that colonized people must first make themselves the subject of recollection. They must critically analyze the results of the influences to which they were subjected by the invader-colonizers. These results are reflected in the behavior, the way of thinking and acting, the conception of the world and society, and the way of assessing the values created by one's own people. The new authentic identity must be reclaimed from all of these influences. This kind of self-analysis on the part of colonized man involves a profound change of personality. It means a de-colonizing of the mind, a liberation from inferiority complexes, and a rediscovery of physical and mental balance. The newly emerging black church must construct its missionary engagement with these critical elements in mind if it is to speak the redeeming and liberating word of the eternal Spirit which became flesh in Jesus Christ. This indeed is the renewed black church "coming of age, " fulfilling the reason for its existence by carrying out its missionary engagement. The Christian "Nova Huta" is here pointing out the way history is moving. It is a sign of the kingdom of God, a preparatory dispensation doing its thing, getting itself together to become an agent of God's universal salvation.

Karl Jaspers, in his book The Way to Wisdom, speaks of a strange kind of historical reality as follows: "The fall from absolutes which are after all illusory becomes the ability to soar; what seemed an abyss becomes space for freedom. Apparent nothingness is transferred into that from which authentic being speaks to us. "[3]

The old traditional black church and its submissive-survival motif lived with its illusory absolutes in the abyss of apparent nothingness supported by its faith in the God of creation as revealed in the Exodus-Sinai event. The renewed black church coming of age is finding new wings to soar, new space for freedom, a redeemed base from which it may make its own authentic response to God. A statement issued by the National Committee of Negro Churchmen on the Urban Mission in a Time of Crisis (1968) reflects some of the things we have been attempting to convey up to this point. The Committee commits itself to the development of a new and creative style of black churchmanship which will emphasize its distinctive task and opportunity. There are three interrelated dimensions for this new style of mission:

1) The renewal and enhancement of the black church in terms of its liturgical (non-European) life, its theological

interpretation, its understanding of its mission to itself, to the white church and to the nation.

2) The development of the black church, not only as a religious fellowship, but as a community organization, in the technical sense of that term, which uses its resources, influence and manpower to address the problem of estrangement, resignation and powerlessness in the political, cultural and economic life of the black community.

3) The projection of a new quality of church life which would equip and strengthen the church as custodian and interpreter of the cultural heritage which is rooted in the peculiar experience of black people in the United States and the faith that has sustained them for over three centuries on these shores. This, in brief, is a description of the newly emerging black church.

This is not to suggest that the description is complete. New avenues and styles for the black church are still being developed and organized by and for the emerging black church. This discussion is only a preview of what is to come. These ideas, aims and aspirations are raw materials that are going to be refined in the mills of our radical self-analysis and criticism, which is an essential part of the urgent effort to gain and reclaim something of value in black humanity and the black church.

This brings us to the unanswered question concerning the black church and its unique possibility in "recasting the human values of our civilization and restoring its humanistic essence." This question is still open for a future answer, one that will come in the light of the validation of the faith of the black church in its attempt to relate meaningfully to the present historical process. There are strong indications that the newly emerging black church will continue to give serious consideration to its mandate to recast the human values of our civilization and to restore its humanistic essence. But, before this can take place, the black church must continue to de-colonize black minds. It must do away with the kind of value system and culture which depersonalizes the essence of being black and being white. This task is absolutely indispensable if we are to provide the kind of authentic situation in which one can confess Jesus Christ as Lord and Savior. For now awakened to the truth that the Gospel means freedom from oppression and freedom to engage in productive creativity, the newly emerging black church will never again submit to spiritual slavery. It will continue to exercise its prerogatives as a liberated and liberating community.

NOTES

1. Harvey Cox, The Secular City (New York: Macmillan, 1965), p. 145f.

2. Malcolm X, The Autobiography of Malxolm X (New York: Grove Press, 1966), p. 313.

3. Karl Jaspers, Way to Wisdom (London: Victor Gollancz Ltd., 1951), p. 38.

RICHARD RUBENSTEIN

THE HOLOCAUST AND RADICAL JEWISH THEOLOGY

The Crisis of Jewish Identity after Auschwitz

However strong the lure of the future may be and however great the impulse to cut oneself loose from a painful past, one nevertheless must do one's hoping in a present moment. If one attempts to detach his present moment from its provenance in the past, one is left with a present that is unreal because it is purely abstract. It belongs to the capacities of human consciousness to be able to do that with one's own past, but if one exercises it, the present loses its content. The present is concrete for us and thus is a basis for expectation about the future only to the extent that we confer to ourselves a present moment by images and thoughts of the past that are held in our consciousness by memory. What we call and claim as our present is always an historical present, a horizon extending from some remembered event of the past through the present instant to a future which is expected in terms of that past. A theology of the present would therefore necessarily be a reflection on a revelatory or theologically decisive event in the present horizon of a community. For Richard Rubenstein, for Emil Fackenheim, Elie Wiesel and many others, the Holocaust, the murder and incineration of six-million Jews by the Nazis, was just such an event. It is for them theologically decisive, demanding a radical decision for all of their believing, hoping, and loving in the future.

In the summer of 1960, just after completing his doctorate at Harvard University where he studied under Paul Tillich among others, Richard Rubenstein went with his family to Holland. It was his first visit to Europe and he spent it vacationing and becoming acquainted with the Dutch relatives of his wife. In the course of that summer Richard Rubenstein witnessed the emergence of the Jewish identity of two of his children. Certainly, this in itself could not have been altogether surprising to the parents of a nine-year-old and an eleven-year-old. It has happened many millions of times in the course of history. But when it happened to his children, Richard Rubenstein witnessed something that made the coming of his children into their Jewish identity a qualitatively different experience from that of their parents and of their grandparents. The fires of the Holocaust were clearly reflected in their new self-awareness. One day he met his daughter on the streets of Amsterdam reading a book. When he asked Anna what she was reading, she showed him her copy of The Diary of Anne Frank. Anna had known that her mother was the same age as Anne Frank and that she had almost been caught by the Nazis. As Rubenstein looked into the face of his nine-year-old daughter, he saw that "an alienation had entered."[1]

In August of that year he took his oldest son for a short tour into Germany. Through a series of chance meetings they found themselves at a briefing held in Düsseldorf by the official Press Office of the Federal Republic of Germany. It had been called to declare the government's acute embarrassment about the recent acts of vandalism that had occurred in Germany against Jewish synagogues. His son sat quietly through the whole proceeding. When they were alone, he began to question his father. His questions moved in a direction that quite surprised his father. The eleven-year-old had understood that it was the purpose of the government of Nazi Germany to exterminate Jews. But he wanted to know about the state of affairs with his own government. Did the government of the United States know about the existence of the death camps? His father affirmed that the existence of these camps was known to our government. The boy then wanted to know whether the government of the United States could have helped the Jews. Rubenstein said that he wasn't sure, but that he did not think so. The next question was, "Well, Daddy, didn't we have German prisoners in the United States?" When he heard the answer that we did have such prisoners, he asked, "Couldn't they have been used as hostages to make the Germans behave?" The father replied that he had no answer to that question. At that, said Rubenstein, "A shadow of alienation entered that eleven-year-old boy which has never left him."[2] From that time on it became a real question for that child as to whether human community would be possible for him with Americans as well as with Germans.

Having been himself the medium for that "dark shadow

of alienation" passing into the existence of his son, Rubenstein knew that he as a father as well as a rabbi had to come
to terms with the Holocaust. As a rabbi it meant coming to
terms with it theologically. It is not surprising then that one
year later he was again in Germany talking with German pastors and theologians and laymen about the theological meaning of the Holocaust. In August of 1961, at the very time of
the closing of the border between East and West Berlin, Rubenstein was in Berlin conducting through an official interpreter an interview with Dean Heinrich Grüber, a German
protestant minister who had been imprisoned by the Nazis for
aiding Jews. Rubenstein's report of this interview in an article, "Jews, Christians, and Magic,"[3] proved to be controversial and was entirely repudiated by Grüber in a letter to
Christianity and Crisis, the journal that published Rubenstein's
article.[4] The substance of the controversial interview was
more fully elaborated by Rubenstein in his book, After
Auschwitz, in an essay entitled, "The Dean and The Chosen
People." This essay is included in this volume because of
its theological significance, yet one might well ask why it
should be included in a context of ecumenical studies which
have as their purpose genuine understanding between Christians and Jews as men of faith.

Quite apart from the question of whether complete and
clear understanding was established and maintained between
Rubenstein and Grüber in the always complicated procedure of
speaking through an interpreter, Rubenstein's essay virtually
marks the beginning of negative Death Camp Theology. That
is the theological negation of the traditional doctrine of election and covenant as held by conservative Jews and Christians,
and as applied by them to the Holocaust and to other great
historical calamities. Rubenstein's radical negation of the
traditional faith represents one of the real alternatives that
looms before any Jew or Christian who genuinely faces the
Holocaust. His account of his interview with Dean Grüber is
very important because in spite of the fact that Grüber has
written that he "cannot recall having a conversation with Mr.
Rubenstein,"[5] it was in the course of his conversation with
this courageous conservative Lutheran churchman that Richard
Rubenstein made his decision with regard to the Holocaust,
which had been haunting him for some time. What was a
trivial, forgotten moment in the life of the Christian had
earth-shaking significance in the life of the rabbi. Because,
as Paul Tillich taught, the shadow of doubt follows all true
faith, Rubenstein's reflection belongs here as a modern "brook
of fire" for men of faith to pass through, if they are able.

Richard Rubenstein is now Graduate Professor of Religious Studies at Florida State University, in Tallahassee.

NOTES

1. Rubenstein's account of his children's reactions to the Holocaust can be found in his essay, "Some Perspectives on Religious Faith After Auschwitz," published in The German Church Struggle and The Holocaust, Franklin Littell and Hubert Locke, editors (Detroit: Wayne State University Press, 1972), pp. 256-259.

2. Ibid.

3. Richard Rubenstein, "Jews, Christians and Magic," Christianity and Crisis, April 30, 1962, pp. 65-68.

4. Letter of Dean Heinrich Gruber, published in Christianity and Crisis, December 28, 1964, p. 266.

5. Ibid. See Rubenstein's reply on the same page.

THE DEATH CAMPS AND THE DECISION OF FAITH

by Richard Rubenstein

Historical Note

I returned to Germany in August 1961 as the guest of the Bundespresseamt to make a two-week survey of religious and cultural trends. I was scheduled to enter Germany on Sunday the 13th, the day of the closing of the border between East and West Berlin. Because of the international situation, I changed my plans and proceeded to Berlin so that I could observe the crisis directly.

The Bundespresseamt was extremely helpful. They arranged a series of interviews for me with religious and cultural leaders. I shall never forget my interview with Heinrich Grüber, Dean of the Evangelical Church of East and West Berlin. He dramatized the consequences of accepting the normative Judaeo-Christian theology of history in the light of the death camps. After my interview, I reached a theological point of no return--If I believed in God as the omnipotent author of the historical drama and Israel as His Chosen People, I had to accept Dean Grüber's conclusion that it was God's will that Hitler committed six million Jews to slaughter. I could not possibly believe in such a God nor could I believe in Israel as the chosen people of God after Auschwitz.

In the winter of 1964, Dean Grüber wrote to Christianity and Crisis denying the words I had ascribed to him. I replied that I did not bear the Dean any ill-will nor did I have any reason to falsify his words. The significance of

---

*This selection first appeared as "The Dean and the Chosen People?" in Reconstructionist magazine, published by the Jewish Reconstructionist Foundation, 15 West 86 Street, New York, N. Y. 10024. It is reprinted here with the permission of the Reconstructionist.

the Dean's assertion of God's Lordship over the death camps is precisely the fact that he was not a Nazi or an anti-Semite but a very decent human being who believed in the historic doctrines of the election of Israel and of God as the final author of the historical drama.

The Dean and the Chosen People

There is an enlarged photograph in the Jewish Historical Museum in Amsterdam which epitomizes much that Jews feel concerning Christianity's role in the "final solution." The picture was taken in Westerbroek Concentration Camp in the Netherlands at a Christmas party celebrated by the SS and their women. Those responsible for the death of over one hundred and ten thousand Dutch Jews took time out of their grisly labors to celebrate the birth of their Jewish God in the very place where they were sealing the doom of every single Jew they could find. The plain fact of the matter is that those who murdered the Jews were, if not believing communicants of the Christian faith, at least men and women whose only exposure to religion was derived from Christian sources. Furthermore, contrary to much supposition, the people directly involved in the murder enterprise were not gutter riff-raff. More frequently than not, they were men with university or professional training behind them. In some instances, former pastors were active leaders of the work of death.

Christian thinkers very frequently point out that Nazism was an anti-Christian explosion which departed utterly from Christian morality. This is undeniably true. It does, however, gloss over the difference between those anti-Christian feelings which are rooted in a competing value system such as Islam, and the anti-Christian explosion of Christians against their own value system. Nazism was an anti-Christian movement. It was, nevertheless, dialectically related to Christianity. It was the negation of Christianity as negation was understood by Hegel and Freud. It could have as little existed without Christianity as the Black Mass of medieval satanism could have existed without the Mass of Catholicism. Assuredly the classic villains of Christianity, the Jews, became the prime objects of extermination of the anti-Christian Christians, the Nazis.

The more one studies the classical utterances of Christianity on Jews and Judaism, while at the same time reviewing the terrible history of the Nazi period, the more one is prompted to ask whether there is something in the logic of Christian theology, when pushed to a metaphysical extreme, which ends with the justification of, if not the incitement to, the murder of Jews. Though there is an infinitude of pain in the exploration of this question, neither the Christian nor the Jew can avoid it.

Given the question of the relationship between Christianity and the holocaust, I considered myself very fortunate when, during the summer of 1961, while I was on a visit to Western Germany, the Bundespresseamt, the Press and Information Office of the German Federal Republic, made it possible for me to visit and interview Dr. Heinrich Grüber, Dean of the Evangelical Church in Berlin, at his home in Berlin-Dahlem. It was my third visit to Germany in thirteen months. The first two visits were private and unofficial. On this occasion the Press and Information Office was extremely helpful in making it possible for me to come to understand something of the complex reality that is present-day Western Germany.

Thousands of Germans could have testified against Eichmann and offered relevant testimony. Only one actually made the trip to Jerusalem to testify. Dean Grüber is a Protestant clergyman with a very long and heroic record of opposition to the Nazis on Christian grounds, and of friendship and succor for Nazism's chief victims. In the end, his courage brought him to Dachau and near-martyrdom. His resistance was especially meritorious because it incurred the possibility of great danger to his wife and children as well as to himself.

Since the war Dean Grüber has devoted himself to the work of healing and reconciliation. He has been instrumental in creating the Heinrich Grüber Haus in Berlin-Dahlem, an old-age residence for victims of the Nuremberg laws. These included Germans who had married Jews, Jews who had converted to Christianity, and a few old Jews who, in spite of the fury which had disrupted their lives, wanted to end their days in Berlin. With public and government support, a very spacious and attractive home has been built for these people who were the very special concern of the Dean.

In addition to testifying at the Eichmann trial, Dean Grüber has been instrumental in fostering the work of reconciliation between Germany and Israel on the political level, and between German Christianity and Judaism at the religious level. At his suggestion, on his seventieth birthday his German friends and admirers contributed well over one hundred thousand marks for the planting of a forest in his honor in Israel. He rejected all gifts. He insisted instead that the money be given to build Israel. He is also active in a German-Israeli organization devoted to the exchange of visits between the youth of the two countries. He has visited Israel three times.

The Dean is over seventy, but there is a healthiness and a heartiness to his person which is noticeable immediately. He has a very attractive and spacious home, something very rare in Berlin today, where, of necessity, apartment-house living is all that most people can hope for. He met me at the door and brought me to his study which was lined with books, a rather attractive oil copy of Rembrandt's Flora, and all sorts of relics and souvenirs of a long and distinguished career. In one corner, there was also a very impressive sculpture of the Dean's head.

After many sessions of interviewing Germans in all walks of life, I had learned to expect the interviewee to undergo a warm-up period before the initial reserve wore off. In the case of the Dean, this was unnecessary. There was an admirable bluntness and candor to his manner which revealed that the man means exactly what he says. This thorough-going honesty was present to the point of pain throughout the interview. It was not a quality the Nazis valued.

The most obvious point of departure for the conversation was the Eichmann trial. He explained that he went to Jerusalem with the greatest reluctance, and only after his name had come up so frequently that he felt he had no decent alternative. He also asserted that he went as a German, a member of the people who had perpetuated the injustice, and a member of the Christian Church which had remained silent before it.

"Did testifying cause you any harm with your own people?" I asked.

He replied that it had not and went on to say that he did not really see much difference between himself and Eichmann, that he too was guilty, that, in fact, the guilt was to be shared by all peoples rather than by Eichmann alone.

"If there had only been a little more responsibility all around, things would have been different. "

He complained bitterly of how the governments of practically every civilized country turned their backs on the Jews, making it impossible for them to leave. He spoke of his own efforts to secure immigration visas and complained of how seldom he succeeded.

I asked him about the Heinrich Grüber Haus. He explained that he had helped hundreds of people, many of whom were victims of the Nuremberg laws, to leave Germany. In recent years some wanted to return. Originally he had founded his home for twenty people, most of whom were Christians who had lost Jewish relatives during the persecutions. He felt that these people deserved a more comfortable life in their remaining years than most old people. It was also extremely difficult to place them successfully in the average German old-age home as many German old people were still bitterly anti-Semitic and would have objected. To meet these problems, he had built, with much public support, this very unique and very beautiful home.

Without being asked, the Dean informed me that he had never converted Jews and did not want to do so now. On the contrary, he wanted Christians to become better Christians and Jews to become better Jews. I quickly learned that the Dean had very decided ideas on what Jews ought to be and how they ought to behave.

Again continuing without being questioned on the matter, the Dean informed me that Germany's Jews today were in great danger. He said that once again Jews are influential in the banks, the press, and other areas of public interest. This surprised me, as I had been informed that there are only eight thousand employed or self-employed Jews in a nation of fifty million.

"The problem in Germany is that the Jews haven't learned anything from what happened to them, " he informed me. "I always tell my Jewish friends that they shouldn't put a hindrance in the way of our fight against anti-Semitism. "

In view of his long established friendship for the Jewish people, I asked him to clarify his statement. He replied that many of the brothels and risque night clubs, for example, are now in Jewish hands, especially those in close proximity to the army camps.

"For hundreds of years, there has been a virulent tradition of anti-Semitism among the Germans. Hitler exploited that tradition for his own ends. It is very difficult for us to wipe it out. After the Eichmann trial, this is one of my tasks. I am involved in one or two meetings a week to help end anti-Semitism, but it is very difficult because of the Jews in prominent positions and those who are engaged only in seeking money no matter what they do."

In reply, I told the Dean of the feelings of many Israelis that one of the most wonderful things about Israel is that there Jews have the right to be anything they want without relating it to the Jewish problem. I put the problem to him in terms of the freedom of every man to make his own life-choices and to pay the price for his personal decisions.

"Look, I don't understand why you are so troubled about a pitifully small number of Jews in shady positions or being interested in making money rather than following edifying pursuits. It seems to me that every person pays a price for the kind of life he leads. Why should Germans be upset about the life-decisions of these Jews unless they are unduly envious or neurotically involved in other people's lives? Must every Jew make himself so pale, so inconspicuous, even invisible, that he will give no offense? Is that the lesson Jews must learn from the death camps, that they must prove to the Germans their pre-eminent capacity for virtue? Wouldn't it seem a far better solution for all Jews left in Germany to leave and go where they could be anything they wished, without worrying about what the Germans thought or felt about them? After what has happened, why should any Jew remain and worry about attaining the appreciation of the German people?"

The Dean was not prepared to let go. He was disturbed at the thought of the few remaining Jews leaving Germany. He felt that I was correct that Jews had as much right to be anything they pleased as the Germans, but he also felt that, after what had happened, they ought not to do these things, as it made the work of ending anti-Semitism so much harder. It was evident that in his mind there was an objective relationship between Jewish behavior and anti-Semitism.

Having asserted that the Jews had as much right to produce scoundrels or scalawags as any other people, the Dean quickly retracted. He spoke of the ancient covenant between God and Israel and how Israel as the chosen people of God was under a very special obligation to behave in a way which was spiritually consistent with Divine ordinance.

"I don't say this about Israel; God says this in the Bible and I believe it!" he insisted with considerable emotion.

The Dean was not the first German clergyman who had spoken to me in this vein concerning Israel. I had previously met a number of others in Berlin and Bonn. All insisted that there was a very special providential relationship between Israel, what happened to it, and God's will, that this had been true in the time of the Bible and that the Heilsgeschichte [salvation history]* of the Jewish people had continued to unfold to this very day. In fairness to them, it should be pointed out that this belief has been shared by the vast majority of religious Jews throughout history. The theological significance of the Zionist movement and the establishment of the State of Israel lay largely in the rejection of Heilsgeschichte and the assertion that Jewish misfortune had been made by men and could be undone by men. For the pastors the conviction remained--it should be said that the conviction has been strengthened--that nowhere in the world were the fruits of God's activity in history more evident than in the life and the destiny of the Jewish people. In each instance I very quickly rejoined that such thinking had as its inescapable conclusion the conviction that the Nazi slaughter of the Jews was somehow God's will, that God really wanted the Jewish People to be exterminated. In every instance before meeting Dr. Grüber, I was met by an embarrassed withdrawal.

Countess Dr. von Rittberg, the representative of the Evangelical Church to the Bonn Government, a charming and learned lady, was one of the German religious personalities with whom I discussed this issue. She had offered the customary interpretation of Israel's destiny as being guided by a special Divine Concern, but she partially withdrew it in the face of my objection.

---

*Editor's addition.

"Theologically this may be true, but humanly speaking and in any terms that I can understand, I cannot believe that God wanted the Nazis to destroy the Jews, " she said.

Her reluctance to follow the logic of her theology to its hideous conclusion, which made the Nazis the accomplices of God, was, humanly speaking, most understandable. I found a similar reluctance in the other clergymen with whom I spoke, though, because I was a rabbi and a guest, there is a distinct possibility that I did not get a random sampling of theological opinion.

The same openness and lack of guile which Dean Grüber had shown from the moment I met him was again manifest in his reaction to my question concerning God's role in the death of the six million, a question which I believe is decisive for contemporary Jewish theology.

"Was it God's will that Hitler destroyed the Jews?" I repeated. "Is this what you believe concerning the events through which we have lived?"

Dr. Grüber arose from his chair and rather dramatically removed a Bible from a bookcase, opened it and read: "Um deinetwillen werden wir getötet den ganzen Tag ... for Thy sake are we slaughtered the whole day long...." (Ps. 44:22).

"When God desires my death, I give it to him!" he continued. "When I started my work against the Nazis I knew that I would be killed or go to the concentration camp. Eichmann asked me, 'Why do you help these Jews? They will not thank you. ' I had my family; there were my wife and three children. Yet I said, 'Your will be done even if You ask my death. ' For some reason, it was part of God's plan that the Jews died. God demands our death daily. He is the Lord, He is the Master, all is in His keeping and ordering. "

Listening to the Dean, I recalled Erich Fromm's description of the authoritarian personality in Escape From Freedom. All the clergymen had asserted the absolute character of God's Lordship over mankind and of mankind's obligation to submit unquestioningly to that Lordship, but none had carried the logic of this theology as far as the Dean did.

The Dean's disturbing consistency undoubtedly had its

special virtues. No consideration of personal safety could deter the Dean from total obedience to his Heavenly Master; this contrasted starkly with too many of his fellow country-men who gave lip-service to a similar ideal but convenient-ly turned the other way in the crisis. Nevertheless, there was another side to this stance which was by no means as pleasant. Eichmann also had served his master with com-plete and utterly unquestioning fidelity. Even sixteen years after the close of hostilities, not only Eichmann, but appar-ently his defense counsel, seemed to feel that such servitude was self-justifying. Furthermore, in both the Dean and his demonic antagonist, the will of the master, in the one case God, in the other case Hitler, was unredeemed by a saving empiricism. Neither man preferred an inconsistency in log-ic to the consistency of accepting the gratuitous murder of six million. In neither individual was there even a trace of personal autonomy.

When Dr. Grüber put down his Bible, it seemed as if, once having started, he could not stop himself. He looked at recent events from a thoroughly Biblical perspec-tive. In the past, the Jews had been smitten by Nebuchad-nezzar and other "rods of God's anger." Hitler was simply another such rod. The incongruity of Hitler as an instru-ment of God never seemed to occur to him. Of course, he granted that what Hitler had done was immoral and he in-sisted that Hitler's followers were now being punished by God.

"At different times," he said, "God uses different peoples as His whip against His own people, the Jews, but those whom He uses will be punished far worse than the people of the Lord. You see it today here in Berlin. We are now in the same situation as the Jews. My church is in the East sector. Last Sunday (August 13, the day of the border closing) I preached on Hosea 6:1 ('Come, and let us return unto the Lord: For He hath torn, and He will heal us; He hath smitten, and He will bind us up'). God has beaten us for our terrible sins; I told our people in East Berlin that they must not lose faith that He will reunify us."

I felt a chill at that instant. There was enormous irony in the Dean's assertion that the Germans had become like Jews. I was listening to a German clergyman interpret German defeat as the rabbis had interpreted the fall of Je-rusalem almost two thousand years before. For the rabbis, Jerusalem fell because of the sins of the Jewish people.

For Dean Grüber, Berlin had fallen because of the sins of the German people. When he sought words of consolation with which to mollify the wounding of his imprisoned church he turned to the very same verses from Hosea which had consoled countless generations of Israel.

He pursued the analogy between Germany and Israel: "I know that God is punishing us because we have been the whip against Israel. In 1938 we smashed the synagogues; in 1945 our churches were smashed by the bombs. From 1938 we sent the Jews out to be homeless; since 1945 fifteen million Germans have experienced homelessness."

The feeling of guilt was very apparent; so too was the fact that for him German suffering appeased and ameliorated this feeling. Everything he said reiterated his belief that God was ultimately responsible for the death of the Jews. It may have been a mystery to him, but it was nevertheless taken as unshakable fact.

The Dean had asserted that God had been instrumental in the holocaust. He had not asserted the nature of the crime for which God was supposed to have smitten the Jews. During the Eichmann trial, Dr. Servatius, the defense counsel, had offered the suggestion that the death of the six million was part of a "higher purpose," and in recompense for an earlier and greater crime against God, thereby joining the modern trial in Jerusalem with one held twenty centuries before. Time was running short. I did not have the opportunity to question Dean Grüber concerning the nature of the enormous crime for which six million Jews perished. His thinking was so thoroughly drenched in New Testament and Prophetic categories that there is little reason to think that he would have disagreed with Dr. Servatius. Stated with theological finesse it comes to pretty much the same thing as the vulgar thought that the Christ-killers got what was coming to them.

At a number of American Protestant seminaries, there have been attempts to study and tone down some of the more patently anti-Semitic teachings in religious textbooks and literature. Similar efforts are today being made within Catholicism. The Jewish declaration of the Vatican Council is the outstanding example. Many thoughtful Christians assert that all men, insofar as they are sinners, killed Christ and that the blame must therefore not be placed on the Jews alone. In the face of a crime so hideous as the holocaust,

decent men recoil and attempt to do what they can to root
out the incitement to further evil. These attempts have
been rightly appreciated in Jewish circles. Yet one is
forced to ask whether there is even the slightest efficacy to
any of these efforts. The fundamental issue transcends the
question of whether Jews are regarded as Christ-killers:
At the heart of the problem is the fact that it may be impossible for Christians to remain Christians without regarding Jews in mythic, magic, and theological categories. Jews
alone of all the people in the world are regarded as actors
and participants in the drama of sin and innocence, guilt and
salvation, perdition and redemption. If the Jews are an utterly normal people like any other, capable of the same virtues and vices, then there is no reason to assert that Jesus
had more than a human significance. The Christian Church
must insist on the separate and special character of the
Jewish people in order that its claims concerning the significance of Jesus may gain credence. As long as Jews are
thought of as special and apart from mankind in general,
they are going to be the object of both the abnormal demands
and the decisive hatreds of which the Dean spoke.

It would seem that as long as there is Christianity,
Jews will be the potential objects of a special and ultimately pernicious attention which can always explode in violence.
Even were all the textbooks "corrected, " there would still
be the Gospels, and they are enough to assure the ever-
present threat of a murderous hatred of Jews by Christians.
Even when Christians assert that all men are guilty of the
death of the Christ, they are asserting a guilt more hideous
than any known in any other religion, the murder of the
Lord of Heaven and Earth. On the Jewish side, we would
say that not only are the Jews not guilty of this deicide, but
that no man is guilty because it never happened. Here
again there is an unbridgeable wall. The best that Christians
can do for the Jews is to spread the guilt, while always re-
serving the possibility of throwing it back entirely upon the
Jews. This is no solution for the Jews, for they must insist that this dimension of guilt exists for no man in reality,
although they might be willing to admit that it exists for every man in fantasy.

What made the visit to Dean Grüber so memorable
and so interesting was the fact that here was a Christian
who had almost died because of his efforts on behalf of
Jews--the Nazis kicked out his teeth and at one point he was
left for dead in Dachau--yet he was incapable of seeing Jews

simply as normal human beings with the same range of failings and virtues as any other group. It may be argued that the Dean's opinions prove nothing, that he exhibited a typically German incapacity to place the concrete, empirical facts of day-to-day life before an overwhelming ideology. There is undoubtedly some truth in this. Nevertheless, the Dean's attitudes, especially in view of what he had done, intensify the question of Christian theology and the death of the Jews.

My visit did suggest one element of hope. Most Americans and Britons simply don't think the way Dean Grüber does. There seems to be something in the German mentality which demands utter metaphysical consistency. This has often been productive of much good. It has resulted in some of the greatest and most imaginative uses of the human intellect. The system of Hegel comes to mind immediately. Nevertheless, the existentialist and pragmatic protests have a validity which can be justified at least on human grounds. Human relations cannot, must not be absolutely consistent with ideological necessities. When they are, life is lost and a dead, murdering logic destroys what it cannot countenance.

Out of my interview I came away with a question for the Jewish community. Can we really blame the Christian community for viewing us through the prism of a mythology of history when we were the first to assert this history of ourselves? As long as we continue to hold to the doctrine of the election of Israel, we will leave ourselves open to the theology expressed by Dean Grüber, that because the Jews are God's Chosen People, God wanted Hitler to punish them.

There is a way out and Reconstructionism has pointed to it. Religious uniqueness does not necessarily place us at the center of the divine drama of perdition, redemption, and salvation for mankind. All we need for a sane religious life is to recognize that we are, when given normal opportunities, neither more nor less than any other men, sharing the pain, the joy, and the fated destiny which Earth alone has meted out to all her children.

We began with a question, whether the Christian Church's attitude involves it in a process which in times of stress incites to the murder of Jews. To this question we must now append a further question, whether the way Jews regard themselves religiously contributes to the terrible pro-

146 / The Contemporary Explosion of Theology

cess.   The tendency of the Church to regard Jews in magic and theological terms encourages the view that the vicissitudes of Jewish history are God's will.   If we accept his theological premises, there is no way of avoiding Dean Grüber's conclusion that God sent Hitler.   But how can we ask Christians to give up these premises if we continue to regard ourselves in this light?   No man can predict the way the matter will end.   There is, however, no doubt that the simple capacity of Jew and Christian to accept their own and each other's humanity lies at the core of any possibility of reconciliation between the two great faiths of the Western world.

ELIE WIESEL AND EMIL FACKENHEIM

THE VOICE OF THE HOLOCAUST

Out of the Silence of Auschwitz

Elie Wiesel and Emil Fackenheim are witnesses to the renewal of the covenant faith of Israel through the experience of the Holocaust. Both European Jews by birth, both felt the scourge of Nazi anti-Semitism. When Wiesel was fifteen years old, he was deported with his family from their home in Hungary to Auschwitz and then to Buchenwald. He alone survived of his immediate family. Emil Fackenheim grew up in Germany where he experienced the outbreak of the Nazi plague. Fackenheim has struggled all his life against the temptation to return towards Germans the same hatred that he received as a Jew in Germany. He has reminded himself and others many times that had he been born a Gentile, he might have been found among the murderers rather than with the intended victims. This compassion for the haters by the hated can be found among many Jews. They were able to see that the haters were most to be pitied for they destroyed their own souls even as they set out to eradicate the spirits of other human beings.

Wiesel and Fackenheim have pursued different careers, yet the fact of the Holocaust has united their thinking and their impact on the Jewish community in Europe and North America today. Wiesel is a writer who commutes between Paris and New York, turning out stories and essays in both French and English. Fackenheim has been a rabbi and a philosopher whose academic career took him from Germany to Scotland, and finally to Canada where he is now teaching at the University of Toronto. What Wiesel and Fackenheim shared in the first instance was an agonizing silence about the death camps. They were Jews of a very profound silence. They could not speak or write about the Holocaust for a long time. They had their thoughts, of course, but if they had uttered them too soon, it would have trivialized the Holocaust. It would have rendered it just another event in the history of modern civilization--one which the world at large is conscious of today, but forgets tomorrow. The silent remembering of the Holocaust by survivors was evidence of its profound religious significance.

According to rabbinical tradition, God spoke to his people in three basic ways. He spoke directly to his people in the Torah, the Law, which was considered as words from the mouth of God. Prophecy was held to be as indirect speaking of God to his people through his chosen instruments. But there was yet another way that God might communicate with his people. The rabbis of old often referred to the will of God as revealed by a Bat Kol. This was a heavenly or divine voice by which the God of the covenant often announced his commandments or his judgments to an individual person, or to a group of people including a whole community, or even to a nation. One of the traditional stories containing a Bat Kol is that of the death of Rabbi Akiba. He was tortured and mutilated as brazen tongs were used to tear his flesh from his body. With his dying breath he uttered the final words of the Jewish confession of faith, "The Lord is one." At that moment a Bat Kol was heard saying, "Hail to you, Rabbi Akiba, that your soul left you with the word 'One'." At this, the angels protested, "Is this the Torah and this its reward?" God then answered, "They have their portion in the age to come," and a Bat Kol said again, "Hail to you, Akiba, you are destined for eternity."[1]

For Elie Wiesel and Emil Fackenheim a Bat Kol, a voice, spoke through the flames of the Holocaust. Wiesel has likened it to the voice of the burning bush at Sinai.[2] Fackenheim calls it "The Commanding Voice of Auschwitz."[3] He has heard it as a commandment for all Jews, because he is convinced that the survival of the faith of Israel now depends upon obedience to that voice.

The following passage from Elie Wiesel's Night, the account of his existence in the death camps, takes the reader to the doors of the ovens as one Jew saw them. The selection from Fackenheim's article, "The Commandment to Hope," is a condensation of his theology of the Holocaust.

NOTES

1. This story is included in the discussion of Bat Kol in
   The Jewish Encyclopedia, Vol. II (New York and
   London: Funk and Wagnalls, 1902), p. 592.

2. Wiesel made this comparison in an address at the International Scholars Conference on The German
   Church Struggle: 1933-1945 at Wayne State University in March, 1970.

3. Emil Fackenheim, God's Presence in History (New York:
   New York University Press, 1970), p. 84.

ARRIVAL AT AUSCHWITZ*

by Elie Wiesel

The cherished objects we had brought with us thus far were left behind in the train, and with them at last, our illusions.

Every two yards or so an SS man held his tommy gun trained on us. Hand in hand we followed the crowd. An SS noncommissioned officer came to meet us, a truncheon in his hand. He gave the order:

"Men to the left! Women to the right!"

Eight words spoken quietly, indifferently, without emotion. Eight short, simple words. Yet that was the moment when I parted from my mother. I had not had time to think, but already I felt the pressure of my father's hand: we were alone. For a part of a second I glimpsed my mother and my sisters moving away to the right. Tzipora held Mother's hand. I saw them disappear into the distance; my mother was stroking my sister's fair hair, as though to protect her, while I walked on with my father and the other men. And I did not know that in that place, at that moment, I was parting from my mother and Tzipora forever. I went on walking. My father held onto my hand.

Behind me, an old man fell to the ground. Near him was an SS man, putting his revolver back in its holster. My hand shifted on my father's arm. I had one thought-- not to lose him. Not to be left alone.

---

*From Night by Elie Wiesel (New York: Avon, 1970), pp. 39-44 abridged. Reprinted with the permission of Hill and Wang, a division of Farrar, Straus & Giroux, Inc., from Night by Elie Wiesel, copyright © 1972 by Elie Wiesel, copyright © 1960 by MacGibbon & Kee, and by permission of Georges Borchardt, Inc., New York, for the British Empire outside of Canada.

The SS officers gave the order: "Form fives!"
Commotion. At all costs we must keep together.

"Here, kid, how old are you?"

It was one of the prisoners who asked me this. I
could not see his face, but his voice was tense and weary.

"I'm not quite fifteen yet."

"No. Eighteen."

"But I'm not," I said. "Fifteen."

"Fool. Listen to what I say." Then he questioned
my father, who replied:

"Fifty."

The other man grew more furious than ever. "No,
not fifty. Forty. Do you understand? Eighteen and forty."
He disappeared into the night shadows. A second man came
up, spitting oaths at us.

"What have you come here for, you sons of bitches?
What are you doing here, eh?"

Someone dared to answer him. "What do you think?
Do you suppose we've come here for our own pleasure? Do
you think we asked to come?" A little more and the man
would have killed him.

"You shut your trap, you filthy swine, or I'll squash
you right now! You'd have done better to have hanged your-
selves where you were than to come here. Didn't you know
what was in store for you at Auschwitz? Haven't you heard
about it? In 1944?"

No, we had not heard. No one had told us. He
could not believe his ears. His tone of voice became increasingly brutal.

"Do you see that chimney over there? See it? Do
you see those flames? (Yes, we did see the flames.) Over
there--that's where you're going to be taken. That's your
grave, over there. Haven't you realized it yet? You dumb
bastards, don't you understand anything? You're going to be
burned. Frizzled away. Turned into ashes."

He was growing hysterical in his fury. We stayed motionless, petrified. Surely it was all a nightmare? An unimaginable nightmare?

We continued our march toward the square. In the middle stood the notorious Dr. Mengele (a typical SS officer: a cruel face, but not devoid of intelligence, and wearing a monocle); a conductor's baton in his hand, he was standing among the other officers. The baton moved unremittingly, sometimes to the right, sometimes to the left.

I was already in front of him.

"How old are you?" he asked, in an attempt at a paternal tone of voice.

"Eighteen." My voice was shaking.

"Are you in good health?"

"Yes."

"What's your occupation?"

Should I say that I was a student? "Farmer," I heard myself say.

This conversation cannot have lasted more than a few seconds. It had seemed like an eternity to me. The baton moved to the left. I took half a step forward. I wanted to see first where they were sending my father. If he went to the right, I would go after him.

The baton once again pointed to the left for him too. A weight was lifted from my heart.

We did not yet know which was the better side, right or left; which road led to prison and which to the crematory. But for the moment I was happy; I was near my father. Our procession continued to move slowly forward. Another prisoner came up to us:

"Satisfied?"

"Yes," someone replied.

"Poor devils, you're going to the crematory."

He seemed to be telling the truth. Not far from us, flames were leaping up from a ditch, gigantic flames. They were burning something. A cart drew up at the pit and delivered its load--little children. Babies! Yes, I saw it-- saw it with my own eyes ... those children in the flames. (Is it surprising that I could not sleep after that? Sleep had fled from my eyes.)

So this was where we were going. A little farther on was another and larger ditch for adults.

I pinched my face. Was I still alive? Was I awake? I could not believe it. How could it be possible for them to burn people, children, and for the world to keep silent? No, none of this could be true. It was a nightmare.... Soon I should wake with a start, my heart pounding, and find myself back in the bedroom of my childhood, among my books....

Around us, everyone was weeping. Someone began to recite the Kaddish, the prayer for the dead. I do not know if it has ever happened before, in the long history of the Jews, that people have ever recited the prayer for the dead for themselves.

"Yitgadal veyitkadach shmé raba ... May His Name be blessed and magnified...." whispered my father.

For the first time, I felt revolt rise up in me. Why should I bless His name? The Eternal, Lord of the Universe, the All-Powerful and Terrible, was silent. What had I to thank Him for?

Never shall I forget that night, the first night in camp, which has turned my life into one long night, seven times cursed and seven times sealed. Never shall I forget that smoke. Never shall I forget the little faces of the children, whose bodies I saw turned into wreaths of smoke beneath a silent blue sky.

Never shall I forget those flames which consumed by faith forever.

Never shall I forget that nocturnal silence which deprived me, for all eternity, of the desire to live. Never shall I forget those moments which murdered my God and my soul and turned my dreams to dust. Never shall I forget these things, even if I am condemned to live as long as God Himself. Never.

COMMANDED TO HOPE*

by Emil Fackenheim

A rabbi in the Talmud once wondered out loud what sort of questions a Jew might be asked at the time of ultimate judgment. That's quite a question. And the answers he gave himself were pretty standard on the whole: Have you been honest in business? Have you sought after wisdom? and so on. But one question was rather startling. One of the questions he'll be asked is, Have you hoped for the Messiah? Now it's an obvious fact that a messianic hope is a part of Jewish religious experience. But is there such a thing as a commandment to hope? Can you be commanded to hope? That's what I think is arresting about the story. And the reason it arrested my attention is that it seems to me, and this is my theme here, that contemporary Jewish experience is such that hope becomes a command. Hope may not be something based on evidence; hope may not be something based on predictability; hope becomes a command. That's what I shall try to develop here.

As I turn to the subject of hope in general, I have to make a few preliminary points. One is the genuine joy that I have that Christian theologians should be turning to the subject, and turning away from what I have considered all along the arid subject of the God-is-dead theology where the proponents could not agree on three subjects: what they meant by God, what they meant by is, and what they meant by dead. I think the subject of hope is a real one; the other one was largely for the newspapers.

---

*This selection, exclusive of the summary, is from the essay "The Commandment to Hope" by Emil Fackenheim, published in The Future of Hope, edited by Walter H. Capps (Fortress Press, 1970). This abridgment reprinted by permission of Fortress Press.
The summary is reprinted by permission of New York University Press from God's Presence in History by Emil Fackenheim. Copyright ⓒ 1970 by New York University.

The subject of hope is not only a real one, but it is also one that brings Jews and Christians perhaps closer together than they have ever been before. If you ask yourself just one simple question, "How come Jews are still around after thousands of years, mostly exiled?" there is only one answer, and that answer is hope. So here there is a tremendous opening for dialog, as the great word is. And, of course, a Jew could not possibly refuse to participate in a discussion of this particular subject--all the more so because we are all in very nearly desperate straits on it.

The central question is: What is the situation regarding the Jewish messianic hope which has persisted stubbornly for twenty-five hundred years? How does it stand today? The reason this question must be asked is that Jews in this very generation have lived through two events which are more startling than any other, certainly since the destruction of the second temple. Nothing much happened for two thousand years except the emancipation. Then two immense events occurred in one generation--the Holocaust and the rise of the State of Israel. I won't talk about the rise of the State of Israel, partly because I don't really feel competent, but I must talk about the Holocaust.

Now any Jew who says that the Holocaust is unique is likely at once to be misunderstood. I've talked about this so often, and I've been misunderstood so often, that I must make at least one point clear; it is painful to me that I've found in the past that it needed to be said. The life of a Jewish child murdered at Auschwitz is no more valuable than the life of a German child who was killed by bombs in Dresden, or a Japanese child who died at Hiroshima. I have to make this very clear because I have been misunderstood many times. And that is not what I mean when I say that the Holocaust is unique.

Why is it unique? Whatever one may say about Hiroshima, its purpose was to win the war. When Eichmann sent trains needed for military purposes elsewhere to ship Jews to their deaths at Auschwitz, this was not a rational goal; this contrary to military purposes. If you then say that there was no rational purpose like winning the war, can one say that there was, perhaps, an irrational purpose, like that of Torquemada, who burned heretics in order to save their souls? Once again, you have to answer, if you have read any of this literature at all, that Eichmann had no desire to save souls. Eichmann, in fact, tried to destroy souls as well as bodies by humiliating people in incredible ways before putting them to their deaths. If indeed one tries to understand what was going on, no matter how many volumes have been written, one must say it was unintelligible because what you have here is not evil done or condoned for certain other purposes, but evil for evil's sake, or, to put it otherwise, the diabolical. The Nazi revolution has been called the "revolution of nihilism," which means destruction for destruction's sake. And if you ask, "Why should anybody want to do destruction for destruction's sake?" I think the closest I can come--only this is not an explanation, and is never meant to be one--is to think of the devil. Anyway, this is the stark brute fact with which we are confronted. My task is to discover whether there is such a thing as a Jewish religious response to it.

Here, too, I am driven to the conclusion (and I say this after many years) that the challenge of the Holocaust is unique. There are some people who have said, "Well, maybe we are just punished for our sins." This, I think, is utterly blasphemous. A million children have been punished for the sins of the rest of us? There are some other people who say, "Well, it must have been God's will somehow, even though we don't know it." I must confess that that is the one time, perhaps the only time, that I feel any kind of sympathy with the God-is-dead theologians. Other people, including Jews in Israel, have said (and this is a terrible thing), "Had it not been for the Holocaust, there would be no State of Israel." And I think it is probably quite true. But it is one thing to say there is a causal connection, and it is another thing to say there is a purpose, as if the one justifies the other. It is a terrible thought, and I think the only reaction one can have is to say, "I won't even consider finding a purpose in Auschwitz because the very attempt to find it is blasphemous."

But, it is one thing to try to give an explanation; it is another thing entirely to seek a response. A religious man is really never concerned with giving explanations. For example, if the Book of Job is meant to explain the problem of evil--boy, is it a lousy explanation! It is no explanation at all. The Book of Job is not an explanation, but a response. How do you live with evil? That is the question. I think explanations belong to science and philosophy, and not to religion at all.

Well, then, what is the content of the response to

Auschwitz? This is the real problem which confronts a Jew.
And there are no precedents of any kind either within Jewish
history or outside it. Martyrs, Jewish or Christian, were
given a choice. Job, who is often quoted in this connection,
died despite his faith. If you think of racism and ask,
"What about victims of racism elsewhere?" Well, then,
racism is the issue, religious faith is not! None of these
categories fit. The one million Jewish children murdered in
the Nazi Holocaust died neither because of their faith nor despite their faith, nor for reasons unrelated to their faith.
They were murdered because of the faith of their great-grandparents. Had these great-grandparents abandoned their Jewish faith and failed to bring up Jewish children, then their
fourth generation descendants might have been among the Nazi executioners, but not among their Jewish victims. Like
Abraham of old, European Jews sometime in the mid-nine-
teenth century offered a human sacrifice by the mere mini-
mal commitment of bringing up children in the Jewish faith.
But unlike Abraham, they did not know what they were doing.
And, also, there was no reprieve. This is the brute fact,
the fundamental fact, the most important thing I have to say.
And this is the fact which threatens the Jew with despair,
because after Auschwitz we can no longer plead ignorance.
After Auschwitz we have to ask if we have the right to bring
up Jewish children, when four generations from now, we
might be implicated in their being murdered. But when I
ask this question of the generation of my great-grandfathers
in Germany, I cannot help but ask the other question: Which
would you rather have their great-grandchildren be, Jewish
victims at Auschwitz or Nazi executioners?

These are some of the terrible questions one has to
confront--moral dilemmas, moral religious dilemmas--for
which there is absolutely no precedent, and which, therefore,
threaten with despair. And, I think, because they are such
terrible questions, it has taken twenty-five years before anyone has started thinking about them. Richard Rubenstein
says, "The facts are all in; now comes the interpretation."
When we have momentous and terrifying events happening to
us, it takes about twenty-five or thirty years to assimilate
them. And I can report of the Jewish community, I think,
as a faithful reporter, that they are only just beginning to
think about the Holocaust. What I think about others, such
as, for example, Germans, I think they haven't begun to face
up to it yet. I would say this is not necessarily a judgment,
because it is such a stunning event. How can you face up to
it? The analogy I like to think of--not that it is an analogy

because there is none--is that the whole generation of Sinai
for forty years was not able to comprehend what happened
at Sinai. And, therefore, the great question that arises for
Jews after Auschwitz is really: Just forget about it? Or,
should you try to cope with it? One thing I say flatly, and
I agree with Rubenstein on this, if Judaism can survive only
at the price of forgetting Auschwitz, then it does not deserve
to survive.

Now, here we have a terrible dilemma, and you can
perhaps understand why the element of clown and laughter
and dancing and celebration is not uppermost in Jewish
thinking at the moment, and why this different witness is
necessary.

What is the response? There isn't as yet any response. When one asks this question, however, one comes
upon a very startling discovery. To me this discovery is
quite startling, and I came upon it only two or three years
ago. By all rights, by all logic of human affairs, in response to this unprecedented persecution, Jews throughout
the world should have used every possibility for disappearing
as Jews. Looking at it from a moral point of view, who
can be guilty of having his children or great-grandchildren
murdered? Looking at it from a human point of view, who
can stand one half of the world not giving much of a damn
about it? This is what the situation was in the thirties.
Yet, what has happened is the very opposite. If nothing
else, I think, the Jewish community is committed to one
thing, and that is survival--which you might say in ordinary
times is not very much. But I will try to show that it is
perhaps the greatest faith the Jewish community has, and
that it transcends the usual distinction between religious and
secular.

In the age after Auschwitz, for any Jew to survive as
a Jew and bring up his children as any kind of Jew, however
half-heartedly done, is itself a monumental act of faithfulness. I am quite sure of one thing, and that is that it has
been a response to the Holocaust. If it had not occurred,
maybe assimilation and disappearance would have been much
greater. Now, how do you understand that? And on this
matter just two or three years ago I was driven to a new
theological thought.

In thinking about the question, Where was God at
Auschwitz?, Buber, the one whom I followed on so many

things for many years, spoke of an "eclipse of God. " An "eclipse" means that a chasm has been created between man and God. Well, in a way, the strange thing about this is that it seems the only thing you can say. On the other hand, if about the most momentous events the Jews have experienced in two thousand years this is what you have to say, does it mean that God is around only when trivial things and nice things happen? Jews never had to say this before. Now, I think this is no longer adequate.

And when I think of the monumental fact of the determination of Jewish survival after Auschwitz, I think that while it is perfectly clear that no redeeming voice is heard in Auschwitz, or ever will be heard, in its unrelieved darkness, a commanding voice is heard. I feel very Jewish on this because the one thing I find missing in the Christian emphasis at the moment on hope is that there must be commandment where there is hope. The emphasis on clear commandment is always a Jewish duty. There is a commandment issuing from Auschwitz. And I would like to give it a general kind of term: A Jew has to be witness against Hitler and all his works. A Jew is not permitted to give Hitler any belated or posthumous victories. And this is possible all over the place.

A Jew might well say, "Well, we will proceed as if nothing has happened; we will forget about the victims of Auschwitz. " You remember that we have records of how in one death camp after another, hundreds arose with no hope except possibly that one might escape. And why was it so important one should escape? So that he would tell the tale. This happened again and again in the Warsaw ghetto and elsewhere. What should a Jew now do? Could he possibly say, "We won't tell the tale. " It would be blasphemy after this.

Number two: Hitler tried to destroy every Jew living on earth, and did his best. For a Jew now to say, "Well, let's disappear; this is why Jews survive, " would also be blasphemy. We are put in the strange position of testifying against the devil by our very existence.

Number three: It is very easy, of course, for a Jew who remembers Auschwitz to be bitter, or to be negative toward non-Jews; if Jews ever in their history were left alone, that was the time. But if one is bitter, one gives Hitler yet another victory, because there is one thing that Hitler tried to do and that is to separate Jews from mankind, and from

Christians in particular. And, I say, to create bonds is to hand Hitler defeat.

The biggest concern of all, and perhaps the most difficult one, is, I think, that a Jew is forbidden to despair of God. Hitler tried to destroy the Jewish belief in God as well as Jewish existence. For a Jew to do Hitler's work on account of Hitler--to say, ''I despair of the God of history because Hitler has proven him to be absent from history''-- would be to hand Hitler yet another victory. Now, this is a very difficult matter, because what to believe and what not to believe is not clear. The commanding voice of Auschwitz is clear, however.

How can one fulfill this commandment? How can a Jew survive as a Jew and witness against Hitlerism, when, unlike Jews before, he knows that this may possibly mean another Auschwitz? I think there is the answer which is expressed in the commandment to hope. I think merely to survive, to exist as a Jew after Auschwitz, is to be committed to hope: to hope because you are commanded to hope, because to despair would be a sin. It is to be commanded to hope that a second Auschwitz will not happen, not for Jews, not for anyone. It will not happen because it must not happen.

You might say there isn't much empirical evidence. The next Auschwitz might catch us all in a nuclear holocaust. But, I think, to give in to the demons of Auschwitz by despair is to do belatedly the work of Hitler.

In summary, what does the Voice of Auschwitz command?

> Jews are forbidden to hand Hitler posthumous victories. They are commanded to survive as Jews, lest the Jewish people perish. They are commanded to remember the victims of Auschwitz lest their memory perish. They are forbidden to despair of man and his world, and to escape into either cynicism or otherworldliness, lest they cooperate in delivering the world over to the forces of Auschwitz. Finally, they are forbidden to despair of the God of Israel, lest Judaism perish. A secularist Jew who has stayed with his God may be forced into new, possibly revolutionary relationships with Him. One possibility, however, is

wholly unthinkable. A Jew may not respond to Hitler's attempt to destroy Judaism by himself co-operating in its destruction. In ancient times the unthinkable Jewish sin was idolatry. Today, it is to respond to Hitler by doing his work.

CONCLUSION

THEOLOGY IN THE NEW DIASPORA

The community of faith, whether Jewish or Christian, has entered into a new diaspora in our time. As diaspora it means that the people of these faiths are scattered, living in relative isolation from one another. As they pursue their everyday tasks in the world, they are aware of themselves as acting outside of the time and place of their respective communities.

In the diaspora after the Babylonian exile Jews lived in relatively small communities scattered throughout the fertile crescent, although there were some notable exceptions such as the large community in Alexandria, Egypt. While those communities were in relative isolation from one another, the individuals within them worked and played very much within the time and the space set by the community. Faith defined the temporal and the spatial limits of the community as sabbath-keeping, and a growing body of customs and rites associated with it increased in significance. Beyond its religious essence, that diaspora can be characterized as geographic and ethnic. Jews living in different places and speaking different languages maintained their religious identity through the Torah and its interpretation in teaching and ritual. The picture that scholars are piecing together from the Dead Sea Scrolls and other ancient sources suggests that Judaism in diaspora produced many different theologies with various emphases, yet all of them bore the characteristics of a common tradition.

The same kind of diaspora occurred to the Christian church as it was getting started. It could be said that Christianity as a religion was formed in diaspora, if one will admit that it was not completely shaped in the relationship between Jesus and his disciples. The war between Rome and Israel that led to the destruction of the temple in 70 A. D. affected Christians, too, especially if they happened to have

163

been born Jews. Many Jewish Christians left Palestine before the outbreak of hostilities, and some of them may have
found their way to Rome before 69 A. D. By the end of the
century there were Jewish-Christian communities scattered
from Egypt to Asia Minor, and there were gentile-Christian
communities from Caesarea throughout Asia Minor and Greece
to Rome. The Jewish-Christian communities still shared
many of the customs of their people, which became a matter
of controversy between Peter and Paul as reported by the
latter in Galatians, chapter 2. As reflected by the Gospel
of Luke, the gentile-Christian communities brought their own
education and background to bear in their interpretation of
the history of Jesus and the early church. The fact that
there are four authorized Gospels in the New Testament and
a collection of letters by different hands, some Jewish-Christian and some gentile-Christian in character, is evidence of
the diaspora condition of primitive Christianity during the
period of time in which the documents of the New Testament
were produced.

    The new diaspora of the late twentieth century bears
many of the same characteristics as the ancient ones. Now
Jewish and Christian communities are scattered throughout
the world, speaking different languages and appropriating in
varying degrees the culture in which they find themselves.
So the new diaspora is also geographic and ethnic in character. But it has yet another, new characteristic that reflects
modern western culture. The community of faith is not only
distributed geographically among the nations of the world, it
is scattered throughout the many sub-cultures that constitute
the modern technological society. The various enterprises
of modern civilization have produced human associations that
have become, for all practical purposes, separate communities. They share a special task, a common technical vocabulary known only to the "in-group. " They proceed according
to common rules and regulations and they have developed
ethical standards for their "communities. " On this basis,
one might speak of a scientific community within a nation, of
a business community, a political community, an academic
community, and also a medical community. In the modern
world a given community of faith is usually scattered throughout these other "technical" communities. It should not be
surprising therefore that faith seeking and employing knowledge for its own purposes should have produced theologies
that reflect the vocabulary and the concerns that govern these
sub-cultures. Teilhard de Chardin's evolutionary theology is
a reflection of the "scientific community, " just as the theolo-

gies of Jürgen Moltmann and James Cone give expression to
the political and social concerns of their respective communities.

What are the important implications of this new diaspora for the community of faith and for theology?

First: not only will every community of faith produce
a variety of theologies; the particular theologies that are produced will tend to be short-lived. There will probably be
many different black theologies in the near future, just as
there will be many different evolutionary or revolutionary
theologies. The power and the lure of any particular theology will depend upon the extent to which the special concerns
and the language of the sub-culture that produced it are appropriated and shared by believers outside of that sub-culture.
In the new diaspora communication between adherents of the
same historical faith will be more difficult since they will be
hindered by the limitations of their respective "technical" vo-
cabularies. In addition to this, members of the same community of faith may find themselves appropriating and discard-
ing, if not always consciously rejecting, several theologies in
their lifetime. An individual may find it necessary to oper-
ate with several theologies at the same time, depending upon
his or her relation to several different sub-cultures. Faith
will be discerned in the continuity that is disclosed between
the various theologies. The result will be greater theological
sophistication on the part of laymen as they are forced to recognize the primacy of faith over theology and so become less
prone to absolutize any particular theology. In short, they
will have a healthy awareness of the limitations of any theology.

Second: theology will be increasingly theology of the
laity, and not for the laity. As the number of sub-cultures
increases, the idea of having clergymen interpret the faith
for each one becomes less and less compelling. Because the
knowledge explosion makes laymen out of everyone in modern
society, those believers who are members of a particular
technical community will ultimately be responsible for asking
and answering the appropriate theological questions raised by
their special knowledge or culture. This is not to say that
there will be no need for rabbis or priests and ministers in
the new diaspora. Clergymen will have the very important
task of conveying the meaning of the historic documents of
their faith in common, everyday language. People may actually come once more to expect that their clergymen will be

knowledgeable in the Biblical languages and in the history of the community of faith. They will leave it to the psychologists, sociologists and scientists to relate the faith to their disciplines. While the translation of traditional faith into the many different languages of modern society may cause many people to despair because of the wide theological diversity and possible fragmentation of the community, others will find it a veritable epiphany of faith as one sub-culture after another "lights up" in its response to ultimate, theological questions.

Third: the proliferation of theologies through the various sub-cultures will not mean automatically that the community of faith will so pervade the whole of modern society as to constitute a hidden numerical majority. On the contrary, the opposite is likely to be the case! The community of faith will find more and more that it constitutes a minority, not only in the society at large but also in each and every significant sub-culture of society. If, of course, the community of faith is itself defined as a sub-culture, one might assume that it constitutes a majority in its own right. But this raises the important theological question of whether all Israel is "true Israel," or whether all are Christians who go by the name "Christian." Most theologians wisely contend that the true or authentic community of faith is hidden in the empirical community called by their historic name, and so they do not believe that the true community can be discovered by human inquiry. The conscious appropriation of, and acceptance of, its minority status may prove to be the most revolutionary ingredient in Christian theology from now to the end of the century. This bears fuller elaboration.

On Entering the New Diaspora:
A Consciousness Change for Christians

In commenting on the possible meanings of the assertion "God is dead," Emil Fackenheim stated that it means among other things "that ... few contemporary men have a meaningful belief in God." He went on to say, "By itself, it at most means that the long association between Christianity and majority opinion is ended: that henceforth Christian faith must choose between minority status and surrender to secularism. For the believing Jew, this choice never existed."[1]

Here Emil Fackenheim, a Jewish theologian, pointed to something that many Christian theologians have still not fully appreciated. The basic social significance of the so-called "death of God" for Christianity is that Christians can no longer assume that America or any other nation or society in the world is really Christian. Increasingly, Christians will recognize that for themselves, for their own basic attitudes toward life, the world, society, other people, they will have to choose between Christian teaching and the basic premises of a modern, secularized society. At the same time they will also come to see how untenable it is to expect that the faith of a minority could ever effectively furnish basic principles for, or even less itself become the principle for, the formulation of the consensus of society at large. It does not follow, therefore, that Christians in the United States will reject or attack the Declaration of Independence and the Constitution, because these documents do not presuppose adherence to the Christian faith. On the contrary, many Christians will be relieved to learn that the Christian faith does not have to assume, much less to carry, that social burden. The current interest of some concerned citizens and scholars in the development of a viable civil religion will pose no particular threat to them once they recognize that the longevity of the American political system and its acceptance by most Americans are ensured because the founding fathers consciously refrained from appealing to Christian dogma and tradition when writing the charters of our liberty. To the extent that these social and historical facts are accepted without rancor and anxiety, to that extent Christians will have entered consciously into their minority status in the modern world. "The majority consciousness" of medieval Christianity will have no more appeal.

Until the early twentieth century a basic assumption among the broad masses of Europe and America was that these continents consisted of "Christian" nations. Then it became apparent to most observers that the state churches of Europe were maintained by their governments with about the same concern that was shown for the great national museums and the other historical landmarks of the respective countries. Probably the event that most clearly symbolized the end of the marriage of Christianity with self-conscious European imperialism was the abdication of Kaiser Wilhelm at the end of World War I as chief of state and as chief bishop of the Evangelical Church of Prussia. From that time on, the churches of Europe, in spite of their official relations with the states of Europe, became self-conscious minority groups. The attack upon Christendom which began in the theological reflection of a lonely Danish theologian in the early nineteenth century was renewed as Søren Kierkegaard's infinite qualitative distinction between God and man found a new and powerful expression in the thought of Karl Barth. Whatever else it was, Barth's prophetic theology, with its conception of the Word of God that comes "straight down from above" and its sharp distinction between the revelation of God on the one hand, and the religions of man including Christianity on the other, was and remains a penetrating criticism of the majority attitude of western institutional Christianity. With the spreading influence of the theology of Karl Barth European Christianity consciously went into diaspora and accepted its minority status. These themes of Barth resounded in the writings of Catholic theologians, most notably in the works of Karl Rahner and Hans Küng, so that now it can be said that after Barth neither Protestant nor Catholic theologians can ever again comfortably play the role of court chaplains to the seats of power in Europe.

Ironically, just as it was coming to an end in Europe, the majority consciousness of Christianity inaugurated one last attempt to create a "Christian civilization" from a base in Protestant America. In his work, A Christian America: Protestant Hopes and Historical Realities, Robert T. Handy tells the story of the abortive effort of the Interchurch World Movement under John R. Mott and S. Earl Taylor to organize the largest and most influential Protestant denominations and nondenomenational associations in a missionary enterprise which had as its basic purpose "to establish a civilization that is Christian in spirit and in passion, the world around, in Borneo as much as in Boston."[2] In 1920 the leaders of this movement, encouraged by the successful battle for prohibition, set a goal of 336 million dollars for the total movement, forty millions of which were to pay the salaries of more than 2,000 full-time workers who had already been hired. Late in May of that year the fund drive fizzled out and shortly after that the movement simply died.[3] In Handy's view, the failure of this movement, the waning interest in revivalism, the defensive struggle to preserve the "Christian sabbath," and the eventual repeal of the Eighteenth Amendment were the final gasps of "Protestant America." The candidacy of Al Smith for the presidency prefigured a new era in American life, one which was to witness the rising influence of immigrants, workers, and Catholics in political life and with that the appearance of a whole new slate of national issues. While acknowledging the problematical character of setting a date for the end of any great epoch in history, Handy suggests that the year 1935 is a convenient date for marking the end of "the Protestant era in American life. "[4] A close look at the evidence does support his judgment, for by that time American Protestantism, whether liberal or conservative, had passed from political primacy in national affairs, while remaining a significant force. After that time, dry Southern Baptists and Methodists had to deal with wet northern Catholics and Jews in the back rooms at political conventions. In fact, America could no longer be called a Protestant Christian Nation.

But facts are often ignored when the minds of men are gripped by an idea inherited from the past. This is especially true when the idea is supported by the experience of a minority. For example, many people living in small towns in America believe that the essential character of America is to be discerned in the life of the small town. This view may be held in spite of the historical fact of urbanization, which has created many near ghost towns in the great plains and elsewhere. As long as small towns continue to exist in this country, the idea will survive that the essence of America is after all the life of the small town. So it will also be with the idea of a Christian America. If in the face of the historical and the social facts it must be conceded that America is not really a Christian nation, many, but not all, evangelical Protestants will nevertheless still cling to the hope of a Christian America and will work to that end. In their view America is not really Christian because Christians have not been faithful in prayer, nor persistent in witnessing to the converting power of the gospel. So, if America is not yet Christian, it still could be. The slogan, "To win the world for Christ in one generation, " can still be heard in evangelical youth rallies and in "Christian crusades. " This old revivalistic slogan has survived to the present day in spite of the fact that nowhere in the New Testament were believers ever promised that they would constitute a majority of the people of the world, nor even of any nation within it. To listen to this talk about the conversion of continents and the world, one would think that Matthew 7:13-14 tells of a broad and easy gate that leads to life, and of a narrow, straight one that leads to destruction, instead of the other way around. Behind the merely apparent minority consciousness of much of evangelical Protestantism and its rhetoric laced with "Christ-against-culture" motifs, there is a majority consciousness which shows through its projection of "the Christian future, " through its demands for censorship of TV and films, and most dramatically through its symbolic endorsement of candidates for the presidency. What other

meaning can there be of the appearance of the President of
the United States at a Billy Graham crusade?

A refreshing exception to this triumphal tendency of
American evangelicalism are the intentional Christian communities, such as the Reba Place Fellowship of Evanston,
and the community at Deerfield, Ill. which publishes the
newspaper The Post-American. This paper is a prophetic
voice against the evangelical sell-out to the American way
of life which they, like William Stringfellow, understand as
the American way of death. In these communities a new,
authentic Biblical prophetism, if not complete realism, has
appeared. It calls for the transvaluation of American values
in terms of Biblical faith taken seriously. [5]

But conservative Christians are not the only ones who
display majority attitudes which betray a lack of realism
about the power and the influence of Christianity to shape the
larger society. Protestant liberal theologians and activists,
in their zeal for what they deem to be the right kind of social
change, have tended to condemn the churches of America for
failing to influence the nation as a whole. While a denomination may be criticized for not doing what is in its power to
do, just as an individual may be, it is unrealistic to think
that the churches of America could ever successfully dictate
social policy to the whole nation. Those social activists who
condemn the churches for not doing this have not fully appreciated the minority status of Christianity in this country. The
reply of the secular institutions to social policy statements
on the part of church assemblies might very well be put in
terms of the German saying, "Clean up your own doorstep
first!" The policy statements that have been produced on the
expectation that the Church should speak to society as a
whole have only enhanced the general impression of the im-
potence of the churches as they are generally ignored. To
the extent that revolutionary theologies aim at prescribing
social policy and erecting social structures for whole socie-
ties, to that extent they too display an unabated majority consciousness. This is not to say that it is unrealistic or foolish to work for social justice, which is every citizen's moral obligation whether he is a Christian or not. It is foolish to think that secular society will ever again accept
"Christian" prescriptions, whether for preserving the status
quo or for revolution.

The impatience of those liberals and conservatives,
who for different reasons stand in judgment over the churches

for not shaping society, is evidence of the lag between the social and political facts of the minority status of Christianity and the conscious appropriation of these facts on the part of Christians. Unfortunately, those who call themselves Christians in the United States and Canada tend to remain in this cultural lag. To the extent that they participate in the older majority consciousness, to that extent they are out of touch with the reality of their situation and are not at all prepared for Christian living and ministry under the conditions of diaspora. They will not even begin to understand the basic task of Christian theology for the last third of the twentieth century. That task is threefold: first, the history of the churches and Christianity must be interpreted so that Christians can readily understand the historical and the social conditions that not only prevented the universal acceptance of Christianity in the world, but also rendered it a minority in those nations where it once was dominant; second, the scriptures and tradition of Christianity must be interpreted so that Christians may find in them spiritual resources for living as a minority in an alien culture; third, the mission and ministry of Christian churches must be reconceived for a minority group's real possibilities in the world. The result of this historical-theological interpretation would best be called a "theology of humility," for it would be based on a clear recognition of the historical and social limitations of the Christian religion, while at the same time affirming the healing and the wholeness inherent in the Christian gospel.

What is required for Christians with majority attitudes is a whole new outlook, a complete turn-about in their thinking. The Biblical word for this is metanoia, the Greek word which has been translated as "repentance." Originally, metanoia meant a change of mind on the part of those who have begun to see the error of their ways. In Biblical usage it came to mean sorrow or remorse for sin against God and so was understood as a sign of the spiritual rebirth of the Christian. While it may have unfortunate or unpleasant connotations for many people, the modern phrase "consciousness change," which came to be widely used in the discussions of Charles A. Reich's The Greening of America, is not an inappropriate translation for metanoia. It conveys the primary meaning of the word which was a change of mind, a whole new way of thinking about one's ways in the world. What may prove to be startling to Christians with majority attitudes is the realization that they will have to radically change their minds about the terms and the conditions under which they

have understood and propagated the Christian faith. To them
it will appear as if Christianity would no longer be Christianity if it would give up the goal of christianizing the nation
and the world. It may be hard to accept the fact that Christianity itself is being called to repentance, but that is what
is entailed in the conscious acceptance of its minority status
in the world.

The new minority consciousness will eventually rami-
fy, bringing about changed attitudes and relations at all levels of Christian life. Individual Christians will find that their
self-consciousness as Christians will not be diminished, but
rather strangely heightened as their spiritual life develops in
an oscillation between periods of relative isolation from, and
renewed participation in, the community of faith. More and
more, the realization will occur to individual Christians that
the meaning of the Christian faith for them, that their own
identity as Christians, will have to be maintained in spite of
the fact that other members of the family and close associ-
ates in the everyday world are not Christians. As the social
pressures for joining and remaining in the institutional churches wane, more profound personal reasons for commitment
to the Christian faith will come to the fore. As monks and
nuns of another era strengthened their faith with the spiritual
uses of their solitude, the Christians of the new diaspora,
whether clergy or laity, will be driven to find ways to make
re-creative use of their isolation from the community of
faith for their spiritual life. What Thomas Merton did with
his solitude in the midst of his community of faith, others
will learn to do on the job or in their own homes outside of
the community of faith. Reading rooms in local public li-
braries, coffee shop counters, park benches, quiet corners
in hotel lobbies will more and more become places for study,
reflection and meditation because these are the places that
permit solitude and privacy while at the same time maintaining an opening out on the everyday world as the sphere of
action. The Christians of the new dispersion will learn to
stand alone, if need be, just as Jews learned to do in theirs.

The gathering of Christians for worship and study will
also take on new significance and so change the character of
corporate Christian life in the family and in the larger public
community where the church has its institutional expression.
The congregating of Christians for worship will less and less
be understood as an end in itself. This is the basic attitude
which thrust the energies of Christians into the erection of
great cathedrals that symbolized the timeless, eternal axis

of Christendom in the middle ages. More and more, worship and study in community will be understood as rejuvenation for the life of discipleship in isolation from the community of faith. The energies of Christians will thus be turned outward on to the secular world. The great buildings and institutions inherited from the past will be viewed and valued more and more from the standpoint of their present potential use for Christianity in diaspora, rather than from that of their past significance.

This new attitude has already found expression in the architecture of some of the buildings advertised by the Stanmar Corporation for churches. In addition to the traditional colonial structures and the more modern A-frames, Stanmar offers a number of attractive smaller building complexes which do not look like churches. These structures are not only built to last as long as the traditional ones, but they are so designed that they could be easily converted to homes, to attractive residential office buildings, or to schools. In the communities where these buildings already exist the Christian church has assumed a dramatically different profile than that projected by Gothic and colonial structures. More reflective of the meeting houses of early America, these buildings are ideally suited for smaller congregations which may eventually fold. They exude an atmosphere of intimacy in which worship and study and common meals can be carried on as part of the normal rhythm of the community's life. Something about these buildings suggests that the members should tarry a while with one another and get to know one another personally before quickly passing out of the door into the everyday world. Families that worship and study together on more intimate terms will inevitably become more involved and more concerned about one another. To the extent that such congregations seek and appropriate in their educational programs an adequate theological understanding of their diaspora condition and mission, to that extent they will exhibit an integrity in style of life and thought with their architecture, which will tell the larger public community that the emphasis here is on the quality of spiritual life, not the quantity.

This is not to suggest that the older traditional structures should be abandoned for the sake of an authentic expression of Christian faith today. That many church buildings will be sold and razed is a foregone conclusion based on present experience in urban areas and in remote rural areas. But many alternatives present themselves before abandonment is necessary. Already a number of urban churches are offering their facilities for rent or free use by secular organizations and associations. Everything from weight-watchers groups, Alcoholics Anonymous, day care centers, schools for the handicapped, to drama workshops are now being conducted in church buildings around the country. By allowing the everyday world into the church buildings, the congregations have made of their own buildings places that open up immediately to everyday life, and so the diaspora condition of the Christian community is experienced within the traditional structures.

What has accompanied these developments is a healthy tendency for the surviving churches to cooperate with one another in educational and social outreach programs and to enter into dialogue with one another in ecumenical meetings. Where the churches are still numerically and financially strong, as in suburbia, the ecumenical associations are relatively few and are usually carried out on a rather superficial level, such as pulpit exchanges and congregational visitations on Sunday mornings as one congregation joins another for worship. In the older suburbs and urban areas ecumenical associations are becoming a serious strategy for survival. Separate congregations are already using the same facilities in many cities. In other places congregations are discovering new vitality and renewed interest on the part of laymen when the churches combine their resources for joint programs in adult ecumenical education and social service in the larger public community.

In Nutley, New Jersey, where the idea for this volume was first conceived in a course on contemporary theology for laymen, six churches and a synagogue cooperated in an ecumenical program of adult education. Subsequently they formed an organization known as The Nutley Ecumenical Council which consists of three lay representatives and one clergyman from each of the participating congregations. The churches represent most of the Protestant congregations in the town and two Roman Catholic parishes in addition to the conservative Jewish synagogue. The council is currently sponsoring the FISH program in Nutley as well as following through with an adult ecumenical school. By including laymen and clergymen in the same body, which elected a Catholic layman as chairman, these churches are hoping to facilitate communication between the participating congregations about those matters of common concern that arise from the fact that they seek to serve the same larger public community.

The council has not replaced the local ministerial association. The idea for the council originated in the association, which views the council as an enabling organization for many of the proposals that may be made by the clergy. While it is still too new to have demonstrated its potential, this local ecumenical council could point the way to the kind of reorganization at the grass-roots level which would give many declining churches a new lease on life, or at the very least, a way to die with dignity.

At the level of international and interfaith relations the changes resulting from the Christian community's conscious acceptance of its minority status might be demonstrated even more dramatically than at the other levels of human association just discussed. What will have the most far-reaching implications historically and socially is the fact that just as white people and white Christians in particular are entering into their minority consciousness, black people in America are entering into their majority consciousness as they begin to identify with the so-called Third World, the peoples of Asia and Africa.

The French playwright Jean Genet gave powerful expression to the historico-psychological significance of this dialectical reversal in his play Les Negres (The Blacks), first produced in Paris in 1959 and later in New York City. The play begins with the whites (black actors with white masks) in positions of dominance looking down on the blacks at the lowest level of the stage. By the end of the play the relative positions of the whites and the blacks have been reversed. The governor and the missionary, the traditional bearers of the white superiority consciousness, find themselves at the mercy of the blacks. Given the existing legislation in India today and elsewhere restricting Christian missions, there is no question but that the dialectical reversal of political power is already a fact in the world. White Christian missionaries have been made aware of their minority status. Christian missionary activity has been compelled by law to remain within the bounds of humane educational and technical services. The law against proselytizing has added a legal limitation to the sociological limitation of white Christian evangelization.

This cannot help but profoundly affect the relations of white Christians and black Christians. White Christians in their identities as white and as Christian will be forced to recognize that their minority status has to do, not only with religious faith, but also with the historical-cultural factors associated with whiteness. Black Christians qua black will enter into their majority consciousness as they seek justice for the economically and politically exploited masses of the Third World. Black Christians qua Christian will still participate in the minority consciousness of Christianity and in that capacity will serve as the fundamental communications link between the Christian churches and the other religious and national communities of the Third World. Just what form or expression this role will assume in the lives of black Christians remains to be worked out by them as they discover their own unique possibilities for service and mission in our time. One thing is clear. In the future, white Christians will achieve no credible communication with the religious and national communities of the Third World concerning their good intentions for the future well-being of the peoples of the Third World until white Christians have demonstrated these good intentions by working for racial and social justice in their own countries.

As for interfaith relations, there is none more important for the future development of Christianity than its relation with Judaism. Here again another dialectical reversal is taking place. Christianity is entering diaspora just as Judaism in one very important respect is leaving a purely diaspora existence. The establishment of the State of Israel is a fact that has created a whole new condition for the Jewish diaspora. For the first time since about 143 A. D. Jews have a choice as to whether or not they will remain in diaspora. This fact gives their diaspora a whole new character. Elie Wiesel may now say, in his poignant paradoxical way, "I am in Jerusalem when I am not in Jerusalem," but the fact that he may go there at any time he wishes has changed the concrete character of his life in diaspora. If he now goes away from Jerusalem in order to be in Jerusalem, he knows his Jerusalem-away-from-Jerusalem better because he has been in Jerusalem. Now Christians are the ones who have no choice but to live in diaspora if they are to live as Christians.

No more authentic evidence of their having entered the new diaspora can be offered by Christians than their acceptance of Jews as brothers and sisters in spiritual community. Such acceptance will indeed mean that metanoia, that repentance, will have happened. Christians will have faced up to the Holocaust and the contribution to it of centuries of Christian anti-Semitism. They will have consciously entered upon the resolve not to repeat the psycho-religious dynamics of anti-Semitism, and so they will have repudiated all missionary activity aiming at the conversion of Jews to Christianity. In the place of the arrogant attitude which said, "We have the true and right understanding of your sacred scriptures," Christians will bring to the encounter with Jews a profound sense of having shared a common but sad history, and so therefore also share a common destiny. If after the hell of Auschwitz, Christians and Jews can establish genuine communication with each other in full acceptance and forgiveness for past evils, then there can be hope for community anywhere in this torn and alienated world. The awareness of the common destiny will be enhanced as Christians begin to draw upon the resources developed by Judaism for living in diaspora. Common worship on the part of Christians and Jews will not be unthinkable. Indeed, in some places it has already happened.

In June of 1971, during the season of Pentecost, there was a joint Ecumenical Conference in Augsburg, Germany of the Kirchentag and the Katholikentag, the Conference of Protestant Churchmen and the Conference of Catholic Churchmen. This joint conference of the two Christian laymen movements had authorized a working group on "Christians and Jews" to present its recommendations to the whole body. In translation, they were:

As a result of the Christian-Jewish Worship Service held in the great hall of the municipal building on Thursday, June 3rd 1971, and the discussions which followed in four groups, we say to the Ecumenical Pentecost Conference:

1. Ecumenical encounters without Jewish participation are incomplete, because without the Jewish roots the Christian faith develops wrongly, unbiblically.

2. Training, worship, adult education and theological education will only rightly meet today's challenges when the self-understanding of the Jewish people speaks authentically.

3. Christian witness is expressed in the joint practical effort of Jews and Christians for greater justice, greater value of persons in the fight against oppression and exploitation. Missions to the Jews contradict this Biblical assignment.

4. The concrete consequence of ecumenical cooperation between Jews and Christians is expressed
also in strategic solidarity with the state of Israel
and its people as also in political involvement for
peace in the Near East. [6]

Wherever these statements become a mandate for Christianity's way in the world, there a whole new configuration, a
new Gestalt for Christianity, will appear. As the former
majority Christianity was conformed to the image of royal
pomp and ceremony when it took over the legal and political
forms of the ceasars, the new minority Christianity will be
conformed to the image of the Suffering Servant and in this
way rediscover, and lift up for spiritual sustenance and theological reflection, the fundamental continuity between Israel
and the church of Jesus Christ.

Ministry in the New Diaspora

Anyone who is still imbued with the attitudes of majority Christianity will be greatly annoyed by any talk of the
conscious acceptance of minority status on the part of the
Christians of America. The idea of a whole new configuration of Christianity as a servant community in an alien culture will undoubtedly be dismissed by unrepentant Christians
as an expression of a defeatist attitude, and a lack of faith
in the power of the gospel. From the standpoint of the new
diaspora Christians, this acceptance is but the realistic beginning on the way to a proper understanding of the power
of God and of salvation as health and wholeness, the unification of body, mind and spirit in the service of God. Until
they understand that this saying of Jesus, "He who finds his
life will lose it, and he who loses his life for my sake will
find it" (Mt. 10:39), applies just as much to corporate structures as to individuals, Christians with majority attitudes
will continue to give themselves to the corporate self-interest
of their particular institutions as a sign of profound commitment to Jesus Christ and his gospel. They will go on asking
young men and women to lose themselves by giving themselves
to the ecclesiastical corporation while turning a deaf ear to
the message of Christ for the church; hence, they will not
understand that a church which is conformed to the image of
Jesus will also be losing itself in order that it may find a
new and meaningful life. For the Christians of the new diaspora the unrepentant majority church and its corporate structures constitute the primary field of mission. Here is where

the biblical word, "... the kingdom of God draws near, repent, and believe the gospel," is falling as the good seed--sometimes by the wayside, sometimes on stony ground or among thorns and thistles, and happily also sometimes on good ground where it is bearing fruit.

What is at stake is an adequate perception of, and hence genuine contact with, the reality of the church in the world. The majority consciousness of Christianity thinks of the church like a mighty army, the so-called church militant, moving from the past to the future in a grand victory march for which only the leadership changes from generation to generation. The witnesses of majority Christianity tend to think of themselves as the vanguard of the movement that will eventually convert the whole world. The Christians of the new diaspora, on the other hand, think of themselves as at the tail end of a movement that has gone the other way--from out of the future into the past. The apostles Peter and James and Paul, St. Augustine, Pope Gregory VII, Luther, Calvin, Zwingli, Cardinal John Henry Newman, Bonhoeffer, Karl Barth, Pope John XXIII, all these names give an indication of the way that the movement has gone before being gathered to the fathers. The Christians of the new diaspora live with a remnant consciousness that is nurtured by their studies in scripture and tradition, which provide them with spiritual sustenance for their life in dispersion and with the basic models or paradigms for their ministry.

When it is remembered that the documents of the New Testament were themselves produced by a church in diaspora, they can be appreciated more readily by a scattered church today. To take but one example, the Gospel of Matthew was probably produced by a Jewish-Christian community living somewhere in diaspora--scholars aren't sure where--about fifteen to twenty-five years after the destruction of Jerusalem in the Jewish-Roman War of 69-70 A. D. While we have no direct evidence for it, it is not unthinkable that the sights and the sounds and the abominable smells of Jerusalem under siege loomed large in the memory of the Jewish Christians of St. Matthew's church who had survived the ordeal. In any case, the basic document suggests that personal abuse, deprivation, and persecution for the sake of the faith were everyday experiences for the members of this community. In the sermon on the mount, those who were being persecuted were particularly addressed:

Blessed are you when men revile you and persecute

you and utter all kinds of evil against you falsely
for my sake. Rejoice and be glad, for your reward is great in heaven for so men persecuted
the prophets who were before you (Mt. 5:11-12).

It is quite possible that the members of St. Matthew's church
living about 80-95 A. D. were persecuted by the Romans on
the one hand because they were Jews, and by the Jewish religious leaders on the other hand because they were Christians. In this connection chapter 6 of the Gospel of Matthew
is very interesting, revealing the basic religious practices
and the basic religious attitudes of the church of St. Matthew.

Three times in this chapter we find the words "... in
secret, and your Father who sees in secret will reward you"
(Mt. 6:4, 6, and 18). They are found only in the Gospel of
Matthew, indicating the special influence of the situation of
the church of St. Matthew. They are connected, interesting-
ly enough, with admonitions about alms-giving, prayer and
fasting. These were the three basic practices of Judaism at
that time. These Christians were obliged to keep these
practices, but with very special qualifications. They were
to carry them out in a way that would make them inconspicuous to others. This special warning at the beginning of the
chapter bears scrutiny: "Beware of practicing your piety before men in order to be seen by them; for then you will have
no reward of your Father who is in heaven." It is possible
that they were to keep their religious practices a secret because it may have been unhealthy for them as a persecuted
minority group to reveal themselves publicly. In any case it
is clear that the Christians in the church of St. Matthew were
admonished not to make a public display of their religious
practices. These practices were to be the Christian's secret
from the world, known only to God and his brethren. If they
took this admonition seriously, it can be said that they lived
in the world as if they were not practicing their religious
faith. One would have to call this a basic attitude, for it
surely must have influenced everything that they did. But is
this to say that there was absolutely no outward sign or indication of their fundamental faith in God? Was there no evidence at all of the ministry of St. Matthew's community for
the world to ponder?

Chapter 5 of the Gospel provides a significant clue
where it reads:

You have heard that it was said 'An eye for an eye,

and a tooth for a tooth. ' But I say to you, Do
not resist one who is evil. But if any one strikes
you on the right cheek, turn to him the other also,
and if any one would sue you and take your coat,
let him have your cloak as well, and if any one
forces you to go one mile, go with him two miles.
Give to him who begs from you, and do not refuse
him who would borrow from you (Mt. 5:38-42).

These rather strange acts in the everyday world seem to
have been for the church of St. Matthew the outward and
visible signs of their faith in Jesus Christ, and not their
particular religious practices of alms-giving, prayer and
fasting. Interpreters in the past have sometimes questioned
whether the church of St. Matthew actually did such things,
thinking that these words point to the moral ideal implicit in
the gospel. But this is to judge the church of St. Matthew
by the tenor of Christianity as it is being lived today and not
two thousand years ago. It is difficult for a complacent majority consciousness to conceive of the Christian life as taking risks for the sake of others every day, yet this was expected of the church of St. Matthew. They lived every day
as if it would be their last and they understood very well the
reason for taking such risks. They believed that the ultimate significance of their lives in this world did not inhere
in their religious practices, in their alms, prayer and fasting, but rather in their ministry to the needy of this world.
According to Matthew 25:34-40, those early Christians expected to be judged in the age to come on the basis of their
having given food and drink to the hungry and the thirsty,
clothing to the naked, and having ministered to the sick and
visited those in prison. In short, the church of St. Matthew
was a community of people who understood ministry, the service of God, as acts of love and kindness to the poor, the
hungry, the downtrodden of this world. Although a church in
diaspora, itself persecuted and very likely in hiding, the community of St. Matthew understood itself as a servant community to the world around it.

Seen in this light the petitions of the Lord's prayer as
we find it in the Gospel of Matthew are words from out of,
and for, a church in diaspora.

Our Father who art in heaven,
Hallowed by thy name.

The community in diaspora lives for the sake of the sanctity

of the Holy Name of God himself. To exist at all, to live
in this world and to celebrate the Holy Name are one and
the same thing. To let all things and all events have their
special significance, which is their reference to God himself,
even though they exist and occur in a world that rejects Him--
this celebration of existence by hallowing the Holy Name is
the hidden center of the church in diaspora. It is the <u>funda-
mental</u> <u>faith</u> of the community.

Thy Kingdom come.

The community longs for the righteous rule of God himself
who will place the justice of earthly rulers on the balances
of his justice. The high and the mighty will be brought low,
the downtrodden will be uplifted. The persecution of the
community of faith will cease and the scattered people of
God will be gathered for the glorious celebration of the Holy
Name before all of the peoples of this world. Thus will the
new age be constituted. This is the <u>fundamental</u> <u>hope</u> of the
community in diaspora.

Thy will be done,
On earth as it is in heaven.

The community asks that God will take their brokenness,
their scattered condition, their shame in persecution, and
use it all for his purposes. That the years of exile are not
being wasted, that healing and wholeness, that salvation can
happen even under conditions where human alienation and de-
pravity are a polluting presence, that the Holy Name can be
celebrated in spite of monstrous efforts to eradicate such
celebration, that is the <u>fundamental</u> <u>confidence</u> of the scattered people of God.

Give us this day our bread for the morrow.

The community prays that it not be trapped in the fleeting
cares of a transitory now. It asks for release from the
perspective of a one-day fly, so that the vision of the morrow of the Holy Name might break into today, that a readi-
ness for the unexpected, unpredictable events of life will al-
low the community to accept new cares and new burdens as
they appear. This openness to the morrow is the <u>fundamen-
tal</u> <u>possibility</u> for life in diaspora. It is the necessary condition for the survival of the community.

And forgive us our debts
As we also have forgiven our debtors;

The community knows that it, too, must be weighed on the scales of God's justice, that it, too, has sinned on its way in the world. Here it is asking for the beam to be taken out of its own eye so that it might see more clearly the mote in another's eye. The way of the diaspora community in the world is the way of not judging, not condeming others. The way of forgiveness is the fundamental love of the community.

> And lead us not into temptation,
> But deliver us from evil.

What is temptation if it is not the impulse to use other people and the things of God's creation for one's own selfish ends? Temptation for the community in diaspora is the moment of forgetting the reason for its existence--namely, its servant role to God and to the world. Here the community asks that it never forget to celebrate the Holy Name by acts of love and kindness to his creatures. Evil is to defile one's own existence and the existence of others by denying the possibility of celebrating the Holy Name. Such temptation and such evil are the dark shadows that follow the flickering light of faith of the diaspora church on its way in the world. The fear of the diaspora church is that it would fall out of the way of serving and into the way of returning evil for evil.

Paradigms of Ministry for the Church in Diaspora

Food for the hungry, cups of cold water for the thirsty, shelter for strangers, clothing for the naked, aid and succor for the sick and imprisoned (Mt. 25:34-40)--these acts are the paradigms of ministry for the church in diaspora. As paradigms of ministry they represent reverence for God and for one's fellow man. In each of them the two commandments upon which all the law and the prophets depend are fulfilled at one and the same time, namely, "You shall love the Lord your God with all your heart and with all your soul, and with all your mind" and "You shall love your neighbor as yourself" (Mt. 22:36-40). In the words of the Lord of the last judgment this meaning of ministry is made crystal clear: "Truly, I say to you, as you did it to one of the least of these my brethren, you did it to me" (Mt. 25:40). There is no genuine love of God that does not also entail love for one's fellow man. But the reverse is also true. There is no genuine love for one's fellow man that is not also an expression of love for God, even if those who perform such acts do not realize it at the time. This is the scriptural basis for what Karl Rahner has called "anonymous Christians."[7] The service of one's fellow men out of genuine concern for their well-being is also loving God. Such acts are the most profound way of celebrating the Holy Name in the midst of everyday life. In this worship of God there is no distinction between the sacred and the secular. It is radically eliminated.

To call these acts of love "paradigms of ministry" is to say that what the Gospel demands is not simple imitation of them, as if they were the only legitimate acts of ministry. Such imitation would mean that ministry is always individualistic, a one-to-one activity. To see them as paradigmatic of ministry is to focus on the dimension common to all of them--on care as the desire to meet human needs. It then follows that whatever is done by a community or an individual to meet human needs is genuine ministry, and so it is also celebration of the Holy Name. Ministry in the new diaspora will mean finding ways to meet human needs as a relatively powerless minority. What constitutes authentic ministry will depend upon the community's developing understanding of human needs as they unfold with the changing human condition in respect to mankind's relation to the earth as well as in respect of the changing relations of men and women with one another in society. Certainly the movement for women's liberation has shed important light on the fundamental needs of women as human beings.

In the spring of 1972, during the presidential primary campaigns, Howard K. Smith gave an editorial comment in which he expressed a rather profound understanding of mankind's changing needs in a developing world. He said that there is one word that could characterize the whole thrust of our civilization for the last one hundred and fifty years or so. That word is "more." Society wanted more of everything. "Now," he said, "the time has come to change our values from 'more' to 'quality' to 'less and better'." He then admonished the current crop of presidential candidates to rise to the challenge of helping America change its values. What Howard K. Smith said of American society at large applies even more so to the Christian denominations of America. The value of "more" has debased the spiritual life of the churches of America as much as anything. St. Augustine called it concupiscence. Renewal or revival will mean seeking ways to improve the quality of church membership, not quantity. It will mean finding creative ways for the churches to serve the people who do attend, who do participate in congregational life, and not to castigate them for failing to attract more people to worship with them.

But this focus on the needs of the people who do come to worship must not result in ignoring the needs of the social fabric of the nation and of international structures. The needs of society at large are still matters of concern for a minority church, but the church must develop a minority strategy for meeting the larger needs. The minority church will find itself working within coalitions of various sorts and concerns, each of which would aim at meeting some need of society at large. The larger institutions of society--government, health care delivery systems, education, etc.--all require special care just because each of these institutions in turn bears part of the responsibility for meeting societal needs. We must pay special attention to them because civil order, physical health and knowledge are all necessary for the process of identifying and meeting basic needs as opposed to non-essential wants and desires of a self-indulgent society. The care of the institutions which care for basic needs will ever be a matter of Christian concern. This means concern for sound government, efficient and just health-care delivery systems, and educational institutions that combine human concerns with technical competence.

But how are things going for these institutions and for the minority churches in relation to them? To ask this question, as it is being asked at the time of this writing--namely, in the context of the national scandal of Watergate and of the 1973-74 energy crisis--seems superfluous. The nation is shocked by the exploitative attitude that seems to have dominated officials within government and corporation managers from the highest levels down in their machinations and power plays for political control and influence in the 1972 election. The great danger of the exploitative attitude is that it infects the political and social structures whose purpose it is to meet needs, not to exploit needs. The exploiters who man the posts of leadership in government and industry turn their bureaus and corporations toward their own interests and the result is an exploitative bureaucracy and corporation enterprise. There is now a great moral vacuum, a need for meeting the needs of the people of the United States and of the world at large. That need for meeting the needs is for the cultivation of the opposite attitude to exploitation--namely, the attitude of care and concern for the institutions whose function it is to identify and meet genuine needs. This is, as it has ever been, a task for the churches. It seems to be patently impossible because it means asking human beings to place community welfare before their own personal interests. This runs directly counter to what might be expected from self-interested persons in power, but this is precisely the prophetic task of the churches in society--to be ombudsmen of the powerless just as Nathan was to David.

Obviously the answer to the question of how things are going between the churches and the institutions of society is "Miserably!" The churches of America continue with their majority attitudes, allowing the ethics of the Gross National Product employed as a standard of value, which means allowing the corporation bureaucratic consciousness to prevail in the denominational structures. Particular social evils such as racial and sexist discrimination are confessed and attacked in places, but even here the GNP morality remains in charge of the acts of confession and repentance. It is usually held that if the churches were not so discriminatory against women and minority groups, they would be more vital and alive and hence growing. The social fact seems to be that precisely those churches that subtly maintain policies of discrimination are the ones that are growing. The prevailing form of Christianity--namely, of most of that large minority who are related to Christian denominations in some active way--is GNP Christianity. Statistics, not qualitative judgments, serve as the basis for evaluation of effectiveness of the congregation as a whole, and of its sub-groups and of the pastoral leadership as well. A massive burden of unreal and so unnecessary guilt is heaped upon the members of those congregations whose statistics fall, or lag behind others of the denomination. The naive judgment that quantity does reflect quality remains at the heart of GNP Christianity.

Meanwhile, the old basic needs of human beings--for food, for clean water, for clothing, for care for the powerless, represented in Biblical terms by widows and orphans-- are beginning to loom large in the world. What would it do to the whole stance and sense of mission of the churches of America were they to understand that the words, "In as much as you did it not to one of the least of these, you did it not unto me" (Mt. 25:45), apply not simply to relations between people living at the same time, but also to transgenerational relations, to what one generation passes on to future generations as to the means for meeting basic needs of food, water, and clothing? What would it do for our personal and family life, for our common public life, if we set as our primary goal to leave to succeeding generations the best possible basic conditions for maintaining a healthy physical, social and spiritual life? Wouldn't it mean repenting in the first place of GNP thinking and the whole value system associated with it? Wouldn't it mean accepting our limits as an economic enterprise and as a society, as well as a religious community within that limited society? Possibly the greatest contribution that the Christianity of the new diaspora could make to society at large is the pioneering act of accepting finite limitations. This would mean among other things eliminating competition within church structures and fostering cooperation as the fundamental alternative to the ethos of competition. It would mean cultivating a whole new Christian ethic that would amount to the transvaluation of the values of the GNP system. It would mean a whole new self-understanding of individuals and of communities in relation to the biosphere, the physical matrix for our kind of organism, and in turn, of the relation of the totality of history and of nature to God.

This new self-understanding of individuals entails a grasp of oneself as part of the eco-system of organic life and it should find expression in a new intentionality pervading the life of the church. The church would be much more intentional about its worship, its study and its service. The new sense of creaturehood would come to expression in the liturgy and in the celebratory moments of life. The agenda for the study of the church would be the spiritual basis for, and the ways of giving expression to, the place of human life in relation to God as the Lord and Giver of life, and to the world as the sphere for the realization of the gift of life. Such celebration would provide the mandate, and such study the necessary information, for the life of service as meeting basic needs within a finite world. Here liberation means first accepting the limits. From that follows the sense of relief that comes with abandoning the pursuit of things and the materialist status-seeking which is enslaving and ultimately self-destructive for human creatures.

Would it mean all this? or Will it mean this? Shall we continue on the GNP path that is leading to destruction or shall we repent of it and take the new narrow and straight way--the way of the diaspora church which is the way of hallowing the Holy Name as the celebration of life in a finite world? Choose your paradigm for ministry, either the GNP church or the diaspora church, and know now that the church history of the last quarter of the twentieth century in the United States will begin with that conscious choice!

NOTES

1. Emil Fackenheim, "A Response to Five Questions," Quest for Past and Future (Boston: Beacon Press, 1968), p. 314. Copyright © 1968 by Emil Fackenheim. Reprinted by arrangement with Indiana University Press.

2. Frank W. Padelford, "Report of Special Committee on Survey I," Standard LXVI (June 14, 1919), p. 1054, as cited by Robert T. Handy, A Christian America: Protestant Hopes and Historical Realities (New York: Oxford U. Press, 1971), p. 188.

3. Handy, Ibid., p. 195.

4. Ibid., p. 213.

5. For further information, write: The Post-American, Box 132, Deerfield, Illinois 60015.

6. This statement was published in the Christians Concerned for Israel Notebook, No. 4, October, 1971, p. 1. The wording of the translation has been altered here for the sake of clarity. Used by permission.

7. Karl Rahner, "The Future Reality of the Christian Life," in The Christian of the Future (New York: Herder & Herder, 1967), pp. 94-96, cites I Timothy 2:4 as the basis for what he calls "the possibility and existence of anonymous Christians" (p. 95).

INDEX

Adenauer, Konrad, 7
Amsterdam Assembly of
  World Council of
  Churches, 4
Augustine, St., 25, 39

Baldwin, James, 117
Barth, Karl, 10, 27, 35,
  72, 168, 179
Bat Kol, 148
Black Theology, 114-118,
  123-128
Buber, Martin, 108, 159f

Cade, Henry, 117-118
Church, 22-24, 43-47, 54,
  Black Church, 120-128,
    163
  minority church, 14-15,
    166-188
  St. Matthew's Church,
    179-183
Cleage, Albert, 116
Cleaver, Eldridge, 116f
Cobb, John, 73, 84
Cone, James, 117, 165
Curtis, Olin, 55
Cox, Harvey, 120

Davies, Alan T., 7
denominations, 23f
diaspora, 14, 16
  new diaspora, 163-188
Dillenberger, John, 12

ecumenical, 9, 56
ecumenism, 12, 14

evolution:
  process conception, 75-79
  Teilhard's conception,
    56-60

Fackenheim, Emil, 5,
  147-148, 155, 166
Flannery, Edward, 6
Future Shock, 2, 25

God, 22, 24f, 27-33, 68-70,
  84-86, 92-99, 104-109,
  153f
Graetz, H., 6
Grüber, Heinrich, 132
  134, 146

Handy, Robert T., 168f
Hardin, Garrett, 61, fn. 16
Harvey, Van A., 10
Hesse, Hermann, 3
Hitchcock, James, 9
Holocaust, 5, 6, 130-133,
  135-143, 156-158,
  176-178
Holy Spirit, 42-47

infallibility, 37-39

Jaspers, Karl, 127
Jesus Christ, 32, 33, 35,
  42, 79, 83, 88, 95, 98,
  126, 128
  Christ, 109-112
Jews, 5-7, 15, 16, 47-51
  135-147, 156, 157-158,
  164

John, Pope XXIII, 7, 36,
    88, 179

Kraemer, Hendrick, 14
Küng, Hans, 10, 11, 39-40

Lonergan, Bernard, 10
Luther, Martin, 100, 179

Marx, Karl, 102, 116
Marxist, 97, 102
metanoia, 171-172, 176
Moltmann, Jürgen, 100-103,
    165

Niebuhr, Reinhold, 4-5, 27
Nietzsche, Friedrich, 3, 116
Nutley Ecumenical Council,
    174

occasion, 71, 76-77
Ogden, Schubert, 73

Parkes, James W., 6
Paul, Pope VI, 36
Pittenger, Norman, 72
Poliakov, Leon, 6
Post-American, 170
Process-thought, 71-86

Rahner, Karl, 11, 40 fn. 1,
    184
Reich, Charles, 171
Rubenstein, Richard, 5
    130-133, 158-159

Schillebeeckx, Edward, 10,
    88-90
Shantung Compound, 21
Smith, Howard K., 184
Stanmar Corporation, 173f
Steppenwolf, 3

Teilhard de Chardin, 54-60,
    101, 164
Tillich, Paul, 10, 12, 22,
    27, 130

Toffler, Alvin, 2
Troeltsch, Ernst, 22

Vatican II, Council, 7-10,
    12-14, 34, 36, 54, 88

Whitehead, Alfred North,
    28, 71-72
Wiesel, Elie, 5, 15,
    147-148, 150-154
Wilken, Robert L., 7